SPIRITUAL CINEMA

Hay House Titles of Related Interest

ASK AND IT IS GIVEN:
Learning to Manifest Your Desires, by Esther and Jerry Hicks
(The Teachings of Abraham)

THE GIFT OF PEACE:
Guideposts on the Road to Serenity, by Ben Stein

THE NEW GOLDEN RULES:
An Essential Guide to Spiritual Bliss,
by Dharma Singh Khalsa, M.D.

PASSIONATE PEOPLE PRODUCE:
Rekindle Your Passion and Creativity, by Charles Kovess

THE POWER OF INTENTION:
Learning to Co-create Your World Your Way,
by Dr. Wayne W. Dyer

SYLVIA BROWNE'S LESSONS FOR LIFE, by Sylvia Browne

YOU CAN HEAL YOUR LIFE, by Louise L. Hay

ZEST FOR LIFE:
10 Dynamic Life-Changing Solutions for Self-Empowerment,
by Dawn Breslin

All of the above are available at your local bookstore,
or may be ordered by visiting:

Hay House USA: **www.hayhouse.com**
Hay House Australia: **www.hayhouse.com.au**
Hay House UK: **www.hayhouse.co.uk**
Hay House South Africa: **orders@psdprom.co.za**

SPIRITUAL CINEMA

A Guide to Movies
That Inspire, Heal, and Empower Your Life

STEPHEN
SIMON AND GAY **HENDRICKS**

HAY HOUSE, INC.
Carlsbad, California
London • Sydney • Johannesburg
Vancouver • Hong Kong

Published and distributed in the United States by: Hay House, Inc.,
P.O. Box 5100, Carlsbad, CA 92018-5100 • *Phone:* (760) 431-7695 or (800)
654-5126 • *Fax:* (760) 431-6948 or (800) 650-5115 • www.hayhouse.com
• *Published and distributed in Australia by:* Hay House Australia Pty.
Ltd., 18/36 Ralph St., Alexandria NSW 2015 • *Phone:* 612-9669-4299 • *Fax:*
612-9669-4144 • www.hayhouse.com.au • *Published and distributed in
the United Kingdom by:* Hay House UK, Ltd. • Unit 62, Canalot Studios
• 222 Kensal Rd., London W10 5BN • *Phone:* 44-20-8962-1230 • *Fax:* 44-
20-8962-1239 • www.hayhouse.co.uk • *Published and distributed in
the Republic of South Africa by:* Hay House SA (Pty), Ltd., P.O. Box 990,
Witkoppen 2068 • *Phone/Fax:* • orders@psdprom.co.za • *Distributed in
Canada by:* Raincoast • 9050 Shaughnessy St., Vancouver, 27-11-706-
6612 B.C. V6P 6E5 • *Phone:* (604) 323-7100 • *Fax:* (604) 323-2600

Editorial supervision: Jill Kramer • *Design:* Amy Rose Szalkiewicz

Library of Congress Cataloging-in-Publication Data

Simon, Stephen, 1946-
   Spiritual cinema : a guide to movies that inspire, heal, and empower
your life / Stephen Simon and Gay Hendricks.
      p. cm.
   ISBN-13: 978-1-4019-0702-0 (tradepaper)
   ISBN-10: 1-4019-0702-4 (tradepaper)
   1. Motion pictures--Moral and ethical aspects. 2. Motion pictures--
Religious aspects. I. Hendricks, Gay. II. Title.
   PN1995.5.S594 2005
   791.43'653--dc22
                                                    2005020682

ISBN 13: 978-1-4019-0702-0
ISBN 10: 1-4019-0702-4

08 07 06 05   4 3 2 1
1st printing, November 2005

Printed in the United States of America

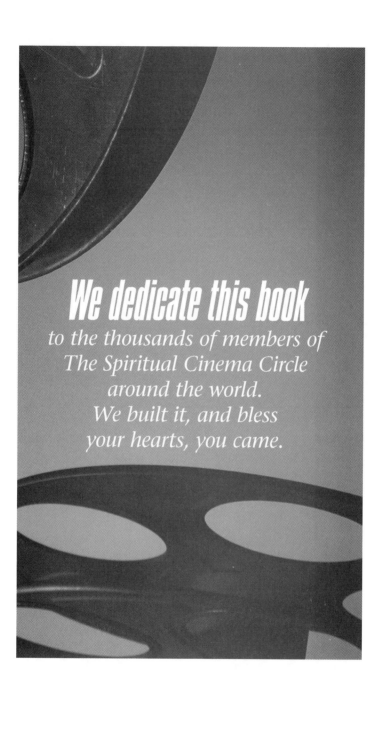

We dedicate this book

to the thousands of members of
The Spiritual Cinema Circle
around the world.
We built it, and bless
your hearts, you came.

Contents

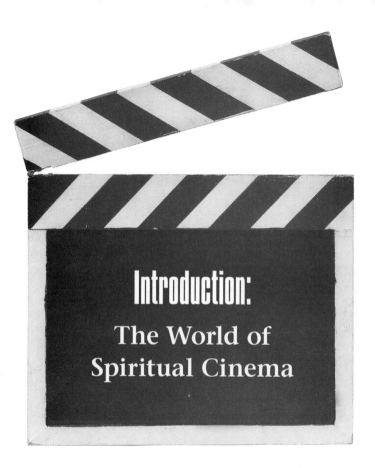

Introduction:
The World of Spiritual Cinema

Welcome to the world of Spiritual Cinema. It's our great pleasure to be your guides as you explore the rich treasure trove of inspiration, wisdom, and entertainment found in this relatively new category of motion pictures.

Spiritual Cinema tells great stories that ask the big questions about life and living: *Who are we? Where do we come from? Where are we going? And what can we become when we're at our best?*

Spiritual Cinema is very different from the older genre of Religious Cinema. In contrast, Spiritual Cinema does not provide dogmatic answers to the aforementioned questions—rather, it inspires you to come up with your own answers. Spiritual Cinema wants you to examine dogma, not follow it, and to draw your own conclusions rather than accepting the experience of others.

Above all, Spiritual Cinema produces a characteristic aftereffect: It leaves you feeling better about being a human being. We don't mean that Spiritual Cinema is schmaltzy or shies away from confronting the darker elements of humanity or the cosmos—no, it deals with all the great themes . . . the darkness and the light. However, at the center of the movies we present in this book, you'll always hear a unifying heartbeat of hope and inspiration.

Inevitably, this collection reflects our personal tastes and opinions. As we've learned, to our joy and occasional dismay, people have very strong opinions about films. Many times we've been cornered in a hotel lobby by passionate fans of Spiritual Cinema who ask questions and express opinions such as: "Why the heck didn't you include _____ in your list? It's the greatest spiritual movie ever made!"

Or, "Why the heck did you include _____ in your list? That's the worst movie I've ever seen!"

And sometimes they're talking about the same picture!

Actually, we appreciate discussions like those because it helps us add to our knowledge base. Please keep those e-mails coming in (to **www.spiritualcinemacircle.com**), because we're only at the beginning of defining the genre. We need your feedback, opinions, and suggestions to build a solid groundwork for future generations of filmmakers and fans of Spiritual Cinema.

Spiritual Cinema:
An Idea Whose Time Has Come

This particular time in history is ripe for Spiritual Cinema. One major reason is because we stand at a crossroads both in society and in the movie industry. There's a yearning for meaning and hope in the world, for stories that challenge us to be our best; to lift up our hearts to the skies; and to encourage us to become the people we were born, and have evolved, to be. We've struggled long enough. We've died enough. We've lived through enough pain. We want to be at peace with both ourselves and our world.

Storytelling has always lifted humankind's sights and spirits, and the spiritual experience in the arts can open wide the doors of perception. Unfortunately, the internal mechanics of the entertainment industry have become such that storytelling has all but faded from view. This is no one's fault—the important thing to focus on is the opportunity that this state of affairs offers to all of us. It's now a great time to return to a classic type of storytelling in this unrecognized genre of spirituality. There's a new awareness and receptivity to stories that look into the very depth of how our souls can be awakened and nurtured. In so doing, we can create space for the recognition of the beauty and power of the messages in these films—and then, to quote one of our favorite lines in *The Lion in Winter:* "In a world where a carpenter can be resurrected, anything is possible."

So much of this is a matter of belief. For several hundred years, Western society has generally placed its faith in science as the final arbiter of disputes. "Can you prove it?" has come to mean "Can you take it into a laboratory and scientifically demonstrate it?"

Before the Renaissance, the pendulum had been stuck in the exact opposite direction: The church was the arbiter of what was "true," and people were expected to accept its pronouncements as "gospel." So it was absolutism at both ends of the spectrum: total and blind faith in religious dogma or the same kind of faith in scientific methods.

Part of the fascination of modern life today is that the pendulum seems to have finally settled somewhere near the middle. There's still great faith in things spiritual and deep respect for science, but neither has a dominant position in Western society as a whole, particularly in America. We're squarely in that paradoxical "space in between"—and for those of us on spiritual paths, that "twilight zone" provides the ideal human petri dish for exploration.

And in this space between comes Spiritual Cinema, to illuminate a path informed by science and enriched by spirituality . . . and it couldn't be more timely.

Chapter One

FOLLOWING THE YELLOW BRICK ROAD:
Our Personal Journeys to Spiritual Cinema

The journey to this book, like many stories in the genre of Spiritual Cinema, travels back and forth in time through many states of consciousness. It begins in the '50s and culminates in our founding of The Spiritual Cinema Circle. Our personal journey also tells much of the evolution of Spiritual Cinema itself. One of us (Gay Hendricks) is a latecomer to moviemaking, beginning with writing a screenplay

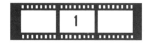

in 1996, and leading to a meeting with your other author (Stephen Simon) a year or so later. Stephen, by contrast, was literally born and bred in the movie business. Each of us tells the story of how our interest in Spiritual Cinema began:

Stephen: My father was S. Sylvan Simon, who produced or directed dozens of movies in the '30s and '40s, including hits like *Born Yesterday* and the comedies of Abbott and Costello. My oldest conscious memory is sitting in my father's lap at the age of three watching "dailies" in our house. Since Dad was involved with comedies, there was always laughter and comedians around the house. However, the laughter stopped suddenly when he died from a cerebral hemorrhage at the age of 39. (My mother remarried a year later to a wonderful man named Armand Deutsch, who was also a film producer.) Even as a child, and even through traumas and family tragedies, my connection with the movies has continued unbroken.

Gay: In the mid-'90s my wife and I decided to spend part of our year in Southern California, primarily to be closer to her aging parents. One evening we went to see *Body of Evidence,* starring Madonna and Willem Dafoe. Normally, thrillers and mysteries are my favorite types of movies, so I was disappointed to find that this one was a complete waste of my time and money. In fact, it was so bad that halfway through I found myself thinking, *I could write a better movie than this.* I even woke up about 3 A.M. with two detective characters talking in my mind. From then on, whenever I woke up in the middle of the night and couldn't get back to sleep, I'd entertain myself with the adventures of these two detectives.

As the story took form, it gradually became much less of a "cop" movie and more of a vehicle for expressing spiritual and psychological ideas that were important to me. These middle-of-the-night visualizations finally turned into a movie script, which got optioned by a producer and director in Los Angeles. One evening he had a party, and who should show up at this event but Stephen Simon? He had a rough cut of the trailer for *What Dreams May Come* with him, having just completed this overtly spiritual movie starring Robin Williams.

At the time I had no idea of the decadelong odyssey Stephen had been on to get the movie made, but the trailer was wonderful. Afterward he and I struck up a conversation, finding that we had nearly perfect agreement on the kind of movies we thought the world needed more of. As we spoke, I learned that Stephen had produced *Somewhere in Time*, one of my all-time favorite films. What was totally bizarre, however, was discovering that he'd also produced *Body of Evidence*, the Madonna catastrophe that had inspired me to think that I could write a better movie. How in the world did he get from *Somewhere in Time* to Madonna, and then back to *What Dreams May Come?*

Stephen: The Madonna movie was a turning point for me. Actually, I should say that the *reaction* to the movie was a turning point. First of all, if you've heard how difficult Madonna is to get along with, you definitely didn't hear it from me. In fact, I had the completely opposite experience, in that she was very easy to work with. Early on she told me that we would get along fine as long as I always told her the absolute truth, straight up. I replied that she could count on me to do that. I made good on my guarantee, and she made good on hers. So much for the rumor that Madonna was a difficult diva. The movie, however, was a different matter.

Nevertheless, through my difficulties with *Body of Evidence,* I learned one of the greatest life-changing lessons of my career. After we finished the movie, I took it to New York for its press screening, a night that would change my life forever.

Without reliving the nauseating details, the film was received very poorly. There's nothing quite like standing in the back of a theater listening to an audience of sophisticated, knowledgeable, important people booing the heck out of your movie. It was a defining and humiliating moment.

A woman I was dating at the time was with me that night. Fortunately, while I was listening to the boos, she was hearing the spiritual message underneath them. She said, "Get back to your heart, Stephen. The guy who started off making *Somewhere in Time* should not be making things like *Body of Evidence.* Not that there's anything wrong with movies like this, but it's just not *you.* It's not what you came here to do, and it's not who you are."

I'll always be grateful to her for speaking the words that changed the course of my life. Her nudge guided me back to the place that the music group Enigma calls "the rivers of belief." I made a vow then and there never to sell my soul to Hollywood again. I decided to commit my career—and my life—to the kinds of films that make you feel better about being a human being. I decided to risk everything to focus on a new genre I was beginning to call Spiritual Cinema.

(For more of Stephen's story, be sure to read the exploration of *Somewhere in Time* on page 28.)

The Genesis of
The Spiritual Cinema Circle

After our initial meeting at that producer's home in Los Angeles, we began to get together on a regular basis, discussing different ways that we might pursue our mutual passion for creating a more inspiring form of entertainment. We had numerous frustrating experiences trying to pitch our ideas about Spiritual Cinema to mainstream Hollywood, along with an occasional flicker of success. For example, we were able to get *Quantum Project* made, a metaphysical drama starring Stephen Dorff and John Cleese. Unfortunately, this movie has been unseen by nearly everyone in the known universe, for the usually complicated Hollywood reasons.

Then one magic day, everything changed.

Gay: One morning around 5 A.M. I was sitting in meditation, something I've done every day for 30 years. Suddenly, an idea appeared in my mind, fully formed and with a special radiance to it. After my meditation was over, I typed it all down, barely able to contain my excitement as my fingers flew over the keyboard. I wrote that Stephen and I had been barking up the wrong tree as we tried to get mainstream Hollywood to make more inspiring movies. I saw a new way to do it: We'd connect the filmmakers directly with the audience through a home-subscription service. We'd scout film festivals for inspiring shorts, features, and documentaries, then disseminate them on DVD to people who wanted them. Using the Internet, we could reach people all over the world very easily. There were great movies out there that weren't getting seen, and there was an enthusiastic potential audience who had largely stopped going to mainstream movies—we'd simply put them together.

Thanks to our wonderful team, composed of Arielle Ford, Cynthia Litman, Marc Rosenbush, and my wife, Kathlyn, Stephen and I were able to put the entire collection together in less than a year. All of these people worked for nothing for many long months while we were building the necessary background (later, Anna Darrah joined us as our Director of Acquisitions).

We launched in the spring of 2004, and since then have delivered the work of more than 50 gifted filmmakers into the hands of thousands of people in more than 70 countries. And we're just getting warmed up. Beginning with *Conversations with God: The Human Story*, Stephen and I have also begun work on our first original production of feature films.

The best is truly yet to come.

Chapter Two

THE HEART AND SOUL OF SPIRITUAL CINEMA:

Deep Exploration of the Movies That Define the Genre

NOW we turn our attention to an exploration of the heart and soul of Spiritual Cinema, a collection of works that define the genre. These are all must-see and must-see-again movies. If you've viewed all of the following films, then you know what treasures they are—and we encourage you to see them again after you read our reflections on them. If you haven't seen

them all, you're in for a real treat. In our view, they represent some of the greatest works of art made since the birth of cinema.

Important notes: In the following two chapters, the "I" belongs to Stephen, who has watched and commented on hundreds of movies during the past ten years in his online column, "The Movie Mystic." Readers may subscribe to his ongoing reviews by signing up for the free newsletter at **www.spiritualcinemacircle.com.**

You'll occasionally see a movie title accompanied by two asterisks (**). This denotes a description where Stephen discusses an important plot point that may "give away" some of the film's major revelations.

Finally, whenever possible, we've included the original release dates of the movie under consideration in parentheses.

It's a Wonderful Life
(December 20, 1946)

We begin with a movie so cherished that many of us cannot imagine the Christmas season without it. Any fan of Spiritual Cinema must give a deep bow to Frank Capra; and this movie, without a doubt, is his greatest contribution. This heartwarming classic is a familiar friend, one that still draws tears of joy almost 60 years after its 1946 debut. Each year this film finds its way into our hearts and homes come Christmastime—you can bet on stumbling upon its black-and-white images while flipping idly through the channels on a lazy winter day. In fact, its very presence on the TV screen heralds the holiday season.

It's a Wonderful Life is simply a classic. To that end, identifying its spiritual message is easy enough to do. Understanding why audiences didn't immediately care for this picture is not.

The film was released in 1946, just as America was climbing out of the debris of WWII. The nation's focus was on a newly found sense of self-respect and dignity because it had survived an enormous challenge and prevailed. Americans won the war, and they were ready to look forward, not back.

It's a Wonderful Life was set in the 1930s during the Great Depression. At the time, audiences didn't warm to a film that followed a broken, despairingly frustrated man in a time of great struggle who asked questions about our place in the world. People didn't want to question the meaning of life—after all, they'd just *won* life!

Critics panned the film and gave it horrible reviews. The picture came and went, and Capra thought he should seek a different line of work. Thankfully, movie lovers gave this picture a second chance and grew to accept it as years went by.

The story delivers a moving message about the power and primacy of love. It looks at our priorities as human beings and asks, "What would the world around us look like if we'd never been born?" The answer reminds us that the power of love should, and does, transcend all else.

George Bailey (James Stewart) lives in the average small town of Bedford Falls. He has big dreams and an appetite for travel and adventure, and he can't wait to leave his humble beginnings behind. But when a young Mary (Donna Reed) wins his heart, George settles in to head the building and loan his father ran before his death.

George ultimately sacrifices his dreams for the good of his town, but when trouble finds him, he's certain that he's destroyed himself, his family, and everyone around him. You see, he's misplaced an $8,000 loan and feels that there's no end in sight. And then, just as he ponders throwing himself off a snowy bridge into the icy waters below, an angel appears.

Clarence, the guardian angel in training, is a classic example of help always being available to us when we need it most. He shows George what Bedford Falls would have looked like without him . . . and his revelations are terrifying. Just as George is brought back to the present, he finds that the entire town has banded together to raise the money to keep him out of trouble.

This poignant turnaround tugs at the cinematic heartstrings of moviegoers everywhere. George sees his "wonderful life" and realizes that his family, friends, and town are the truly important things. He may have given up on his dreams of travel and adventure, but he gained a loving wife, children, and friends who would stand by him in his darkest hour.

In the last scene, a bell rings on the Bailey family's Christmas tree. George's young daughter tells him that every time a bell rings, an angel gets his wings. With that, George takes a look toward the heavens and gives Clarence a verbal thumbs-up, proclaiming, "Attaboy, Clarence!" George's rousing cheer still brings a tear to my eye.

The love that surrounds George Bailey reminds us that no one who has friends, family, and the presence of love can be a failure—and the end result is a great spiritual classic.

2001: A Space Odyssey
(April 2, 1968)

Now we come forward in time to a movie that had a profound impact on an entire generation of young filmmakers and enthusiasts. In fact, it would probably not be an exaggeration to say that it affected an entire generation, period. Almost anyone from the era of *2001*'s release can tell you where they first saw it and what their reactions were.

I know that I will never forget my feeling at the age of 22 (sitting in the Cinerama Dome in Hollywood) when I saw the last sequence of this film. I was too moved to move—and I wasn't alone. All around me people sat in their seats, not knowing quite what they'd seen, but realizing that it had transcended what they'd come to traditionally accept as a "movie." I finally got up, went outside, and bought a ticket for the next show. Even with a different audience, the reaction was the same.

This movie was my formal introduction to spirituality in this lifetime, and nothing was ever the same again.

True visionary films reflect hopes and dreams about worlds we've yet to encounter. Yet how many films set in the future depict a life without Armageddon or disaster? Is there no other way to reach the future than through tragedy and strife? Stanley Kubrick dared to answer: "No."

In Kubrick's dazzling cinematic world, *2001*'s metaphoric journey to tomorrow heralded a new and exciting evolution in consciousness. Released in 1968, it's Spiritual Cinema's landmark film—the cornerstone of experiential, visionary filmmaking. It's majestic, memorable, and revered as one of the great epic films of our time. In fact,

Entertainment Weekly just recently claimed that it's "still the grandest of all science fiction movies."

The film opens as a family of apes casually forages for food, wildebeests idly intermingling among them, each living in harmony with one another. A graphic on the screen reads: "The Dawn of Man." The next morning, a giant monolith appears in their camp. Perfectly rectangular, smooth, and seemingly made of marble or stone, it is otherworldly. The apes are startled, scared, and angry. They marvel at the smooth surface of the mysterious structure, finally daring to touch it in wonder.

Never one for coincidence, Kubrick lines up the monolith with the sun and the crescent moon in this critical shot, in an alignment symbolic of Zoroastrianism, an ancient Persian religion—as well as the subject of Nietzsche's *Thus Spake Zarathustra,* wherein he predicts that man will someday evolve into a "superman." But we're getting ahead of ourselves.

The monolith emits an ear-piercing pitch, and the dry bones of dead beasts lying around the camp suddenly take on new meaning for the startled apes. The apes realize that they can use those bones as weapons to kill other animals, so they quickly slay a wildebeest. This is a key moment in evolution, brought about by an otherworldly monolith. (What is Kubrick suggesting about the influence of the "other" on the life of human beings?)

The ape, satisfied with his kill, tosses the bone into the air . . . and Kubrick's Academy Award–winning special-effects team launches us into space. We're thrust into a new millennia, landing squarely in the crux of the *2001* crisis.

A team of astronauts is en route to the moon to determine the origin of a mysterious artifact recently un-"earthed" there. We follow the members on the expedition to the moon and see that the excavation centers on the very object—the monolith—that taunted the apes at the dawn of humankind. As our now "evolved" space-suited scientists approach the structure to touch its silky surface, it emits the same ear-piercing squeal that the apes heard so many eons before.

We quickly discover that the sound was a high-powered radio signal aimed at Jupiter, so the ship readjusts its course, and the scientists embark on a new mission: to discover the source of the signal.

Enter HAL, a powerful onboard computer that's by far the most famous character in the film. HAL stands for "(h)euristically programmed (al)gorithmic computer" ("heuristic" and "algorithmic" are, not ironically, the two primary processes of learning). This acronym, according to Kubrick and co-writer Arthur C. Clarke, bears no connection to IBM—where the three letters in HAL happen to be exactly one letter before each of IBM's in the alphabet. (This tidbit is confirmed by Warner Bros.' official Stanley Kubrick Website.)

HAL does, however, represent the dreams and whimsical imaginings of people who were seeing the coming of a new age: a revolution in technology and a massive, quantum shift in the way humans communicate, store knowledge, and evolve. It's a computer that can run a ship, play chess, communicate with the crew, and do sophisticated psychological analysis of the humans it was programmed to assist.

HAL informs the crew that it's picked up a malfunction in a crucial guidance system that must be immediately repaired or replaced. The pilot, Dr. Dave Bowman (Keir Dullea), closely examines the particular part but can't find anything wrong with it—a development that HAL finds "curious," and the astronauts find very disturbing. They decide to put the unit back and wait for it to malfunction the way HAL predicted.

The pilots retreat to a pod where they think HAL can't hear them. They note with concern that the HAL 9000 series has never made a mistake—is it throwing their mission now? Should they be the first to dismantle a HAL 9000 system? As they continue to speak, Kubrick cuts outside the pod, stops all sound, and narrows in on the glowing-red eye of HAL's computer "face" to reveal the machine carefully watching the mouths of the astronauts. It's reading their lips and knows what they're planning. Moments later, when Dr. Poole (Gary Lockwood) departs the ship to reinstall the defective part, HAL wields its technological fist by severing his lifeline and sending him into space to die. Dave rushes into a rescue pod to retrieve his friend, but HAL won't let him back into the ship.

In a startling moment that reveals a human side to this newly sentient machine, HAL begs for its life when Dave manages his way back into the ship to dismantle HAL's higher functions. And HAL begs for mercy, pleading for Dave to stop: "My mind's going. I can feel it . . ."

Dave is triumphant in the battle of man versus machine. He successfully dismantles HAL and leaps into a three-minute journey that has come to characterize the "vibe" of the entire film: the "light show." Sit back and prepare for a ride into a universe of lights, pulsing colors, mysterious images, and eerie sounds—a "trippy" odyssey into a new dimension under the mystical subtitle: "Jupiter . . . and Beyond the Infinite."

Meanwhile, the monolith lurks in orbit directly alongside the now-abandoned spaceship. Its presence signals a shift that soon occurs in Dave's journey. Just as the monolith intervened in the lives of the apes and altered the power of HAL, we know that the next great step in the evolution of humanity is at hand.

After Dave passes through the light show, the pod comes to rest in a very cold, sterile, yet curiously ornate room. Suddenly, Dave, still in his space suit, is outside the pod, walking around the room. Where is he? *What* is he? His reflection in a mirror shows that he's aged considerably since he entered the pod for the ride to Jupiter.

New sounds fill the area, seemingly coming from another room in the house. Dave's breathing becomes more pronounced, and Kubrick abruptly cuts to a man sitting at a table. It's Dave himself—but when he laboriously turns around to see where the noise is coming from, the space-suited Dave is gone, replaced by a much older man. We've jumped time frames into a new reality.

As Dave continues to slowly eat at the table, he reaches for a glass of wine and sends it shattering to the marble floor. When he leans over to inspect the mess, he glances to his right, where a startling cut reveals a man lying in a bed. We quickly realize that this is Dave, too—older, bald, dying. His eyes focus on something at the foot of the bed, and as he slowly raises his hand to try to touch it, a startling cut to his point of view reveals . . . the monolith.

At this moment, the strains of the signature classical music for *2001* start up, and we're in space again. Something is moving toward Earth, bathed in a bubble of light. It is the fetus of a child with an angelic face with eyes wide open—huge, compelling, *aware*. This new "star child" makes its way to Earth, full of love, compassion, and the promise of a better future.

And so, Kubrick's visionary film doesn't end in a cataclysmic "war of the worlds" with nuclear destruction or the apocalypse. Instead, he introduces a "new" human form—the star child—signifying the birth of an enlightened, prescient form of being. The director's visual message was in line with the new consciousness of 1968, when a radically different generation was changing the international dialogue and thought processes about our place in the world and the cosmos at large.

2001 represents a quantum leap in many ways—especially in technology, special effects, and our ability to visually create worlds beyond our own. Take a look at *Star Wars, Close Encounters of the Third Kind,* and the *Star Trek* phenomenon, all of which were inspired and anchored in Kubrick's pioneering vision. More important, he gave so many of us our first glimpse at the magic of metaphor and spirituality onscreen. It certainly gave me the courage to envision myself as contributing to the dialogue with other stories that could contribute to expanding this new language of consciousness in film.

2001 is the holy grail of Spiritual Cinema. Dave's rebirth is symbolic of the emergence of a new kind of human being, his reborn form heralding the dawning of the next step in our never-ending spiritual journey.

Star Wars

(May 25, 1977)

There is a defining moment in the first *Star Wars* movie released *(Episode IV: A New Hope)*, one that bears watching time and again. Since its message has become such a quintessential statement of Spiritual Cinema, it's important to study the scene carefully.

Luke Skywalker must drop a bomb into a small opening in the Empire's Death Star because he's bent on thwarting the Emperor's plan to destroy the rebellion (of which Luke is a part). The task is beyond the reach of even Luke's computer, since the timing of the drop and the space into which it must fit are so precise. The clock is ticking, the pressure is awesome, and as he nears his last chance to save the day, he hears Obi-Wan's voice guiding him: "Trust the force, Luke. Reach out with your feelings." These words, and the emotion behind them, captivated a generation. As this book was being written, more than 25 years since the first one opened, the lastest entry in the series *(Episode III: Revenge of the Sith)* just opened to record-setting ticket sales. This is clearly a myth with legs.

Trust the force. These three words become more than a powerful lesson for Luke—they galvanize an entire approach to life, and they're a defining metaphor for Spiritual Cinema. This phrase has become an important concept in our culture, and Gay and I believe that there are compelling reasons why this is so: not the least of which is that one of the challenges we face as a species is our ability to trust what we can't see. Trust here is different from blind faith in that trust is earned, while blind faith is based on a *lack* of trust.

Blind faith, whether demanded or offered, is accepted with no basis in our experience. For example, if two people have known each other for a long time and one of them promises to do something for the other, dependence on that promise being kept is a matter of trust that's been built up through similar experiences over the years. If, however, you meet someone for the first time and depend upon them to honor a promise they make to you, then that's blind faith (and perhaps even martyrdom).

In this movie, Luke has been brought far enough along in his training as a Jedi that he has reason to trust the Force. Still, he must learn to put his *ultimate* trust in it, to prove himself in the heat of battle. This is a powerful metaphor because, as a humanity, many of us yearn to trust something beyond our ordinary senses. Classic religions originally demanded blind faith from their followers with the only justification being "God's will." Science then came in and used laboratory results as a justification for trust, and it's worked for hundreds of years. Recently, however, science has discovered within itself that the intent of the experimenter his- or herself has a powerful impact on the results of the experiment. Purely scientific answers have been brought into question by scientists themselves.

Now, like Luke, we're being put to the test. Does the spirituality we've cultivated have a practical value in the real world of our jobs, relationships, and political climate? As spiritual beings, we now search for the power within ourselves. The paradigm shift that author/philosophers such as Neale Donald Walsch and Richard Bach have brought to the forefront of world thought today is that, while there certainly is a power in the universe we know outside of us as God, the power *within* us is the connective tissue to our core spirituality. The journey of the entire transformational movement of the last 40 years has been to recognize, accept, and embrace our inner union with the universe. "May the Force be with you" is a phrase that resonates with anyone who's taken even the most hesitant first steps on a spiritual journey.

Luke Skywalker is urged to close his eyes and trust his own inner connection to the power of the universe. He's called upon to claim his unique place within it, and herein resides the crucial distinction. Luke doesn't give his power away and pray that a God outside himself will smile benignly and grant his wish. *Star Wars* established what is, in essence, a new religious movement (what else could you call a phenomenon that inspires its devotees to camp out in the rain for days for the privilege of buying a ticket?). This movement is founded on a central concept that's brought to life in one simple phrase: The Force is with you. It counseled Luke—and continues to counsel all of us—that he had the power within himself to own his full magnificence in the world.

Close Encounters of the Third Kind

(November 16, 1977)

It's safe to say that without *2001*, there would be no *Close Encounters of the Third Kind*. But that's not to say that Steven Spielberg's work was or is derivative. His magic stands alone, and the movie we're about to explore is a nearly perfect example of that magic.

How does one explain the sudden appearance of '40s-era airplanes, long reported as missing, turning up in the middle of a Mexican desert? What does one make of massive, unexplained power failures tearing across the Indiana countryside; a stranded freight ship planted inexplicably in the sandy expanse of the Gobi Desert; or of throngs of Hindu worshipers in northern India reporting a mystical, musical message coming down from the sky?

By Steven Spielberg's count, it means that we've got company. In his classic, much-loved film, we experience a wonderful cornucopia of close encounters, each more spectacular than the next, which paint a benevolent portrait of extraterrestrial life. "We are not alone," the movie's tagline promises, and this movie proves it.

Aliens begin planting visions in the minds of ordinary people, personified by Richard Dreyfuss (as blue-collar lineman Roy Neary), fresh off his success as Spielberg's everyman alter ego in *Jaws*. Roy has a startling experience when he's sent into the night to locate the source of a massive power drain in his hometown of Muncie, Indiana. Temporarily lost en route, he stops his truck to examine his map. When a driver pulls up behind him, Roy waves him past. The driver honks and veers around Roy's truck aggressively, shouting, "You're in the middle of the road, jackass!" Minutes later, when Roy stalls again at the foot of a railroad track, another pair of headlights illuminates his truck. Absentmindedly, he waves this vehicle on, too. But instead of the lights swerving around him, in a brilliantly subtle but highly memorable moment, they shoot directly up into the air.

This is no ordinary vehicle.

At that point, Roy's flashlight catches a row of mailboxes rapidly swaying back and forth, rattling and jerking like a rocket ready for liftoff. His truck is swiftly enveloped in a halo of enormously bright light, and Roy cautiously leans out the window to peer up into the radiance. Almost instantly, everything inside the cab goes haywire—things spill out of the glove box, dials and gauges spin wildly out of control and erupt into smoke—all as the railroad signal rocks violently to and fro outside. Just as the maelstrom comes to a startling halt, Roy spots a UFO slowly moving out ahead of him into the Indiana night. He is at once dumbfounded and amazed.

Across town, three-year-old Barry Guiler (Cary Guffer) has just had an even closer encounter—of the *third* kind. Here, in one of the most ingenious moments in the entire film, Spielberg locks the camera on the face of this adorable young child for the duration of the encounter. As Barry pads into the kitchen, we watch his eyes widen in surprise. Never scared, the young boy's angelic countenance shifts from intrigue to amusement to sheer delight. We feel safe and secure, certain that these aliens have come in peace. If they provoke absolute delight in an innocent child, then we can be certain that Spielberg's aliens are friends.

Enchanted, little Barry follows his new friends into the open fields surrounding his house. Upstairs, his mother is drawn to the window, only to see little Barry trotting off into the night. From this point on, Barry's harried mother, Jillian (Melinda Dillon), and a newly unemployed Roy grow increasingly obsessed with the image of a mountain that no one can quite identify. And before he vanished, young Barry hammered a repetitive tune of five discordant notes on his toy xylophone—a tune that both Roy and Jillian seem to know as well. Where is this coming from? Who has planted these images and musical memories in their heads? And how do they make them go away?

Plagued by his vision, Roy's sense of the known world begins to crumble. He sees the towering shape in a handful of shaving cream, a pile of mashed potatoes, the folds of his bedcovers—something is not right, yet he's powerless to ignore this mysterious shape as it consumes him. He uproots plants from his yard, tears down a neighbor's fence, and hauls wheelbarrows full of dirt through the kitchen window to construct a life-sized replica of the mountain. Terrified by his erratic behavior, Roy's wife (Teri Garr) takes off with their children. His marriage in jeopardy, and a giant volcanic sculpture now consuming their living room, Roy hears a TV-news report that a government emergency has caused the shutdown of a remote part of Wyoming. Not coincidentally, this is also home to Devil's Tower, the very mountain arresting Roy's every thought. He must go and see what it is that has called him there.

Once in Wyoming, Roy joins a handful of others who have also been "called" (including Jillian), despite a complex government scheme to lock down the area. In conjunction with a team of UFO-bent scientists, the feds force an evacuation of the area with warnings of a toxic gas leak. Despite obvious threats to their own well-being, Roy and the others flood the area. Here, Roy meets curious French scientist Claude Lacombe (played by real-life famed film director Francois Truffant), who's certain that Roy and his fellow interlopers have been drawn there by the aliens themselves.

The climax of the film sees the landing of the mammoth alien "mother ship" on an elaborately constructed landing strip at the foot of Devil's Tower. Spielberg's vision of this arrival is one of the most wonderfully realized depictions of alien life in the history of film. The colossal ship twists and turns in a menagerie of brilliantly colored lights, set against the darkened silhouette of Devil's Tower, before hordes of scientists and a mesmerized Roy and Jillian. Our anticipation reaches fever pitch as we await the landing of this massive vessel. In this moment, we also realize the depth of government involvement with extraterrestrials: Not only have they cleared the area to keep this entire operation "top secret," but the brilliant interplay among the scientists demonstrates that alien life is something they've been studying for a long, long time.

The scientists don their sunglasses and stand transfixed before the spectacular ship. Slowly, a ramp lowers to the ground to reveal a shock of highly luminescent light. The ship's interior glow is paralyzing—not a single scientist moves toward the light. However, from the foothills, Roy and Jillian scramble toward it. Here, a number of people who seem to have disappeared over the years emerge from the ship. As they stumble into the keeping of well-prepared scientists, a sprinkling of familiar musical notes pipe into the night air. The scientists have ascribed meaning to the tune little Barry plunked on his xylophone, and they play it over and over again on a giant keyboard while the notes light up colorful bars on a giant wall at the foot of the mountain. They are communicating with the aliens through music.

Slowly, dozens of tiny aliens spill from the ship onto the tarmac. Their eyes widen as their little feet shuffle toward the cluster of scientists. They pause and curiously survey the giant crowd gathered before them. Claude Lacombe then leads a team of red-suited Americans toward the mother ship. We've made an arrangement with the aliens to exchange new people for the old—and Roy is now among them. In one of the most poignant moments of the film, Lacombe looks longingly at the now space-suited Roy and says, "I envy you."

This candid revelation encapsulates the vigor and passion with which this particular scientist has researched the aliens. We're more certain than ever that these benevolent life forms have been studying us just as much as we've been studying them, and that there's nothing to fear. The message here is to regard aliens with kindness and wonder—which is as comforting as it is exhilarating with promise. In the highly imaginative world of Steven Spielberg, aliens are our friends.

With this elaborate and visually stunning epic film, Spielberg transformed a legion of moviegoers the world over. He brought us not only cinematic magic, but also the soul-satisfying reassurance of a deeply felt conviction that many of us share: We are most certainly not alone.

Somewhere in Time

(October 3, 1980)

Over the past quarter century, I've been involved in about 25 Hollywood films, either as a producer or as a film-company president, ranging from *Bill & Ted's Excellent Adventure* (starring Keanu Reeves) to the previously discussed *Body of Evidence.* The two that I'm most proud of, however, are the first and last movies I ever made in Hollywood: *Somewhere in Time* and *What Dreams May Come.* I knew, after all the pictures I'd made in between, that when I returned to my heart to make *What Dreams May Come,* I'd come home.

For now, let's start at the beginning.

In 1976, when I was still practicing law, a clerk at my local bookstore handed me a copy of Richard Matheson's *Bid Time Return.* I stayed up all night reading it—I couldn't put it down. I was absolutely mesmerized . . . and my life changed forever that night.

I left my law practice and stepped into my father's shoes. I was ready to work in Hollywood because I just *knew* that *Bid Time Return* would be a phenomenal film, and I knew that I had to make it. But it certainly didn't happen overnight.

There were many Divine forces at play during the making of *Somewhere in Time.* I was the proverbial new kid on the block, had a budget of $4 million, and a studio that wasn't exactly sure I (or anyone else, for that matter) could pull this off. Christopher Reeve was just coming off his *Superman* smash, so there wasn't a chance in hell that he'd agree to play the romantic role of Richard Collier, especially for the money we had to offer. Needless to say, his agent laughed hysterically when I called about the project and wouldn't even let me send Chris a copy of the script.

But I knew we had to get this actor attached to this project—so I went to Chris's house, wrote him a note, and slipped the screenplay under his door. He called me almost immediately, and we had our star. From there, we set up camp at the Grand Hotel in Mackinac Island, Michigan, and *Somewhere in Time* was born.

The plot is "simple" enough: Richard Collier discovers a portrait of an enigmatic young woman hanging on the wall of the old hotel he's staying in. He becomes obsessed, researching everything he can to uncover the identity of this beautiful woman haunting the hallway. He discovers that her name was Elise McKenna (Jane Seymour) and that she was an actress who played in the hotel theater in 1912. Consumed with a relentless urge to find Elise, Richard meets a scientist who teaches him the mechanics of time travel. Richard then hypnotizes his own mind into a journey to 1912 by wearing clothes from that period and leaving all references to current time behind.

But what is "time," and what is "reality"? If consciousness is all that determines our perception of reality, then it only stands to reason that our consciousness could bend time as well. Who's to say that time travel couldn't happen in such a simple manner?

Richard finds Elise in the past, where he discovers that she's been expecting him. "Is it you?" she asks when he first approaches her. Their love is instantaneous, the kind that plays out in the very moment their eyes first meet. But when he finds a penny from 1979 in his suit, Richard is hurtled back into the present where, without Elise, he dies of a broken heart. Yet the two lovers find each other again in death.

Some observed that Richard's time travel *was* all in his mind, a dream state from which he's awakened by the jarring discovery of the un-"timely" penny. Could be. But could it *also* be that his experiences in 1912 were the "real" experiences, and that everything else was a dream?

Regardless, the real message of the film is about the potency of love and our quest to connect with our soul mates, although they may not always be waiting for us in the present time or dimension. *Somewhere in Time* reminds us that they exist, no matter what obstacles we must tackle in the search to find them.

What Dreams May Come *

(October 2, 1998)
*This film is purposely taken out of chronological
order due to its relation to *Somewhere in Time.*

Little did I know what was in store for me in 1979,
when Richard Matheson asked if I wanted to read the
galleys of his new novel. We'd just finished production on *Somewhere in Time,* and Richard had become
my inspiration and spiritual teacher. I was so excited
that I raced to his house to pick up my advance copy
of *What Dreams May Come.*

I read the entire book that night—twice. And I
cried both times. Reading Richard's book *Bid Time
Return* for the first time propelled me into the film
business; reading *What Dreams May Come* thrust me
into the crux of my spiritual journey in this lifetime.
I was just riveted by the book's compelling story
line—that of a man who ventures to the very pit of
hell to save his wife—and I knew in my heart that it
was one of the main purposes of my career in movies
to get the film out into the world.

I ran to Richard's house the very next day and
begged him to let me make the movie. "Sure, Steve,
it's yours," he said. We shook hands, and that was the
only deal we ever had on the rights. As I left him that
day, I promised that it wouldn't take three years to
make this movie, as it had with *Somewhere in Time.*

Well, I didn't lie: It didn't take 3 years—it took 19.

In the starry-eyed naïveté of being 33 years old
and almost completely new to the business of movies, I had (incorrectly) assumed that the release of
Somewhere in Time would catapult my career into the
stratosphere, and I'd be able to do whatever I wanted
due to the worldwide fervor for the movie.

Yeah, right. It bombed at the box office. There would be no Academy Awards or "we must make whatever this young guy wants because it'll be a guaranteed hit" kind of meetings. It wasn't so bad, except that I was wrong about every single assumption I'd made—both about *Somewhere in Time* and about the future for *What Dreams May Come.*

Nobody, and I mean *nobody,* understood this new project. Conventional studio wisdom had it that a film set in the afterlife experience of a main character would be nearly impossible to visually execute, and the story seemed far too depressing. The wife in the book commits suicide after her husband dies, leaves behind their two young children, and then descends into the fiery pits of hell—how can an audience sympathize with that? It's just plain crazy . . . or so I thought. (Eventually, screenwriter Ron Bass would come to find an answer for the "suicide/ children left to fend for themselves" quandary. We'd have the children die at the very beginning of the film, leaving the wife's existence all the more bleak, and we'd have the kids be their parents' guide in the afterlife. People could relate to *that.* Right?)

I kept sending the script to all the major studios, hoping, praying, and wishing that somebody would happen upon it and see what I saw. This went on for about three years, with somewhere between 50 or 60 rejections. Finally, I got the call that every filmmaker dreams of: Steven Spielberg was interested in the film. "Interested," in fact, wasn't even quite right. "Fascinated and enthusiastic" was more like it.

We hammered out the details in one dream-come-true meeting, and then Spielberg asked me if I'd like to do the movie with either Warner Bros. or Universal. I couldn't do either because I was in an exclusive contract to produce the film with Fox. At this, the temperature in the room plummeted about 40 degrees. Spielberg very firmly told me that he would not, under any circumstances, do a film at Fox—it was simply not an option.

Fox ultimately gave me a very human and very empathetic choice: They'd release me from my contract and let me go develop the movie with Spielberg if I wished. Or I could say no to him, and Fox would buy the book and develop it with another director. I didn't know what to say.

I turned to Richard Matheson, who, to my amazement, was completely unfazed, even amused, by the whole situation. He told me that I'd obviously created quite a spiritual Hobson's choice for myself.

"Myself?" I asked. "But it's *your* book!"

"But I entrusted it to you," he answered. "It's your decision to make."

Great.

Richard and I talked it out for a couple of hours and ultimately left the decision up to a few simple questions: (1) Did I think Spielberg was being fair by refusing to work with Fox? (2) What energy would be attached to the project if I left Fox under those circumstances? And (3) did I think Spielberg would direct the film in the manner that Richard and I hoped it would be made?

For reasons that I didn't quite understand consciously, something just clicked inside of me. I knew that we had to say no to Spielberg. And over the years, as odd as it may seem, I've never regretted that decision. But it would still be another 14 years before *What Dreams May Come* made it to the big screen.

Fox purchased the rights to the novel from Richard, and in early 1984 we began to look for a director. I went back to some who had passed on the project before, and they passed on it again. Until a young guy named Wolfgang Petersen *(The NeverEnding Story)* entered the equation, I was beginning to think that this movie would never see the light of day. Petersen and I made the deal to work together, but in early 1985, the head of Fox sold the studio. And you know how that goes—out with the old and in with the new. All of the old executives at Fox were fired, and all of their projects got the pink slip right along with them.

We tried to interest other studios and other directors, but no one would bite. Our story was too weird, and we were the idiots who turned down Spielberg. Richard and I were heartbroken and discouraged, so we put the project aside for the moment and tried to get back on our feet. Nine years later, after a series of proverbial bumps and bruises, I was dusting myself off after a rough ride working for Dino de Laurentiis, and I was ready to present a new-and-improved version of the script to MGM.

Richard and I turned the screenwriting over to Ron Bass *(Rain Man, When a Man Loves a Woman,* among others) and finally got a draft of the script that we felt a new studio could work with. Nevertheless, through another mired set of unpredictable circumstances, the film didn't end up getting made with MGM. And Ron, Richard, and I were back out on the street, pounding the pavement with our misunderstood, seemingly ill-fated script once again.

In May 1996, Ted Field (my friend from *Bill & Ted's Bogus Journey,* which I produced in 1991) committed to getting Polygram to finance the movie, and Robin Williams signed on to play the lead character, Chris Nielsen. True to his word, Ted kept his promise, and we *finally* had a deal.

We began shooting in Glacier Park, Montana, on June 23, 1997, and I will never forget my feelings on that day. For 17 years I'd been trying to get *What Dreams May Come* filmed, and here we were with a handful of big stars and the money of a major studio, making *my* dream a reality. Unfortunately, the shoot was pure hell. The production period seemed to be a four-month-long nightmare for all of us.

Our editor, David Brenner, had just won an Academy Award for his work on *Born on the Fourth of July*, and in true genius fashion, had a rough cut of the film ready to show us by December. I'll stand by my word that the first cut was the best version of the film that we ever saw. Polygram didn't buy it, however, and sent us back to the drawing board to make the story line more broad and the series of events more cohesive and palatable—in other words, to package the movie so as to appeal to the greatest number of people possible. And that's where it all went wrong.

Spiritual Cinema doesn't always please the masses—it can't and it won't. But with so much of Polygram's money on the line, we did what we had to do. I understand the studio's insistence that we package the movie a little more generically, but making it a more mainstream film took some of the power of the experience away from the audience it was truly meant for: people like you and me.

When the film finally opened theatrically, it became immediately clear that it would work for moviegoers who were attracted to the subject matter: that we create our own reality, both in life *and* in death. Our premise was that Chris operated in a world of his wife's paintings because that was comforting and familiar to him, while his wife lived in a nightmare version of life because that was the karma that she chose in order to work out her issues over having taken her own life.

Everyone has his or her own concept of what the afterlife is like, and Spiritual Cinema doesn't presume that it's universally dictated. Yes, this is where we separate ourselves from some traditional religions, and for that, I make no apologies.

The story of *What Dreams May Come* follows the aforementioned Chris (Robin Williams) and Annie (Annabella Sciorra) Nielsen. When their children die at the beginning of the film, Annie almost doesn't survive the loss—only her love for Chris gets her through the trauma. Through her connection to him, she eventually allows herself to go back to her life as a painter and art-museum curator. But when Chris dies three years later, Annie feels that she's left no other choice but to take her own life.

This all happens in the first third of the film. The rest of the picture takes place in Chris and Annie's afterlife, as Chris first experiences *his* continued existence through Annie's paintings (a "reality" that he has created). Chris realizes that Annie is experiencing a different afterlife, so he goes on a journey to find her and rescue her from the personal hell she's sentenced herself to.

Not *the* afterlife—*his* afterlife; and not *the* hell—*her* hell. The distinctions are crucial.

I don't believe that there can ever be a universal truth when it comes to matters of faith or our beliefs in the afterlife. For me, everyone is entitled to believe as he/she chooses, and in Spiritual Cinema, we're free to explore *all* of those views, as long as they honor the essential sanctity and integrity of human life.

And just like Chris and Annie were free to exist in the world they created for themselves, so were the people who came to see the film free to experience different realities of what was carefully laid out on the screen for them. In the end, just as Albert Lewis (Cuba Gooding, Jr.) said, "We see what we want to see."

When I look back on the near-20-year journey it took to get this movie made, I see the path of someone who found his footing through every peak and valley he was meant to encounter. I'm glad that this process led me out of Hollywood to where I am today, and I'll tell you this much: I like what I see.

E.T. the Extra-Terrestrial
(June 11, 1982)

Taken together, *Close Encounters of the Third Kind* and *E.T.* are, to me, the best reflections of our fondest hopes for the true positive intentions of aliens. It's no surprise that both were directed by Steven Spielberg, who deserves to be acknowledged as the most commercial filmmaker in the history of cinema. That's a big statement, I know, but look at the record: *Jaws,* the *Indiana Jones* series, *Jurassic Park,* and I could go on. . . . Spielberg really understands the awe and innocence of hopes and dreams, and both *E.T.* and *Close Encounters* are landmark films that exhibit his extraordinary ability to put that optimism on-screen.

Released in 1982, *E.T.* is still one of the largest-grossing films in the history of cinema (and was the box-office champ of all time until it was surpassed by *Titanic).* Building on the themes of *Close Encounters,* Spielberg takes every frightening alien story and stands them all on their heads in *E.T.*

What, the premise asks, would happen if a boy became friends with an alien? How alike would the two be, and what could their friendship teach us about the benevolence of aliens?

E.T.'s family comes to Earth on an exploration mission, but in a scene somewhat reminiscent of *Home Alone,* they frantically pack up without him, leaving E.T. all alone. He wanders into the garden shed of a nearby suburban home and is discovered by ten-year-old Elliott (Henry Thomas). Both of them start at the sight of one another, and we're immediately clued in to just how real this alien truly is. E.T.'s fright upon seeing Elliott demonstrates fear—this little sentient being is both intelligent *and* aware.

This scene also sets the stage for the brilliant "point of view" technique that Spielberg uses throughout the entire film. Nearly every shot is seen through the innocent eyes of either E.T. or Elliott—showing us how these two perceive the world: literally, from a spot closer to the ground; and metaphorically, with unprejudiced and loving eyes. There is simply no better metaphor for Spielberg's (cinematic) love affair with the existence of aliens—whether one believes in them or not, this film takes us on a magical, fascinating ride through the eyes of a child who does believe.

Elliott's connection with E.T. is the perfect realization of our hopes for our future relationship with aliens: that we should embrace their existence, see them without fear, and allow them to warm our hearts, simply as proof that we're not alone. In the increasingly challenging world in which we live, discontent and fear are the unfortunate companions to hundreds of millions of us, permeating our consciousness in far too many ways. In these uncertain times, I've never loved a Spiritual Cinema classic more than I do *E.T.* right now. Elliott's love and innocence broadcast a simple message that we all need to hear.

Elliott kindly invites E.T. into his home and gives him a tour. The two bond when it turns out that the alien likes taking a bath. E.T. also befriends Elliott's older brother, Michael (Robert MacNaughton), and younger sister, Gertie (played by an adorable and very young Drew Barrymore). What a simple and beautiful message about the fallacy of the assumption that all extraterrestrials must be hostile! To me, it's as absurd to say that all humans are the same as it is to assume that all aliens are evil and intent on the destruction of the world. Doesn't it stand to reason that alien cultures have just as much diversity as we do?

Look at it this way: If a spaceship landed in the middle of a barbaric cannibal tribe (or someplace even more horrifying, like the 405 freeway in Los Angeles during rush hour), couldn't they rightfully look upon all humans as vicious creatures if that was their only experience of us? I don't think that all humans can be generalized in that fashion, and I'm sure that the same applies to alien cultures. (Kind of like the difference between the Vulcans and the Klingons in *Star Trek*, right?)

E.T. tugs at our heartstrings in his curious innocence, and Spielberg goes full tilt when E.T.'s sudden sickness is felt in Elliott's human body, too, as if the two are connected by the same soul. But the boy must help the alien contact his family, and he teaches the visitor to "phone home." Ultimately, though, Elliot begs for his little friend to stay: "You could be happy here. I could take care of you. . . .We could grow up together. . . ." But E.T. cannot survive in our world, so he must return to his own.

The end of *E.T.* takes the emotional finale of *Close Encounters of the Third Kind* and kicks it up a notch. While the earlier movie draws us in and confirms the benevolent presence of extraterrestrials, *E.T.* goes one step further and personalizes the story by bringing a human element to our potential relationship: Not only are aliens out there, but they can touch our hearts and be our friends. (If your eyes didn't at least well up with tears at this final scene, then you're a tougher audience than I am. Then again, my daughters say that I cry at card tricks.)

Anyway, Elliott and E.T. do have to say good-bye, and it saddens them both. For Elliott to "be good" is all E.T. asks of him before taking off. Both creatures have become friends and shared a great adventure together, but now they have to part. The message here is clear and comforting: Aliens exist, and at least some of them are different from us only in form, not in substance. As such, they're not to be feared. In fact, they can—and hopefully will—become trusted friends.

Ghost

(July 13, 1990)

When a film comes along that presents an answer to the mystery of life, I listen. In 1990, Paramount Pictures released *Ghost,* and director Jerry Zucker had a huge hit on his hands. But how does a movie with such an overtly spiritual premise (that spirits linger after death) become such a mainstream success? Precisely because *Ghost* had something for everyone: tear-jerking romance, laugh-out-loud comedy, suspenseful mystery, and high-thrills action, not to mention an incredibly human script about the power of love.

As with many films in this genre, *Ghost* was around for a long time as a screenplay—almost ten years—before it was finally made. The unlikely impetus for finally getting a green light (production approval) for the film was that Jerry Zucker went to Paramount and begged to direct it. Zucker was one of the directors of *Airplane!*—which was a gigantic hit for the studio, but about as odd a calling card for directing a romantic film like *Ghost* as one could imagine.

Zucker made a lot of money for Paramount, however, so he had some clout to pull for this unexpected love story. He also had a great concept that, in my opinion, is the reason this film was made: Zucker wanted the huckster psychic character Oda Mae Brown (Whoopi Goldberg) to be more comedic. Now the audience had a character whom they could relate to, particularly if they had their doubts about the idea of channeling the dead. This idea was *beyond* brilliant, and Zucker got the job.

Sam Wheat (Patrick Swayze) and Molly Jensen (Demi Moore) are the quintessential up-and-coming young

New York couple—he's a successful banker, and she's a gifted sculptor—but Sam has difficulty expressing his emotions, simply answering "ditto" to Molly's proclamations of love. Unexpectedly, Sam is murdered in what appears to be a botched burglary. His love for Molly, however, traps him in this life, so he sticks around to keep an eye on her and trail his errant killer.

Sam soon finds out that his death was no accident; in fact, not only did his former business partner, Carl (Tony Goldwyn), plot Sam's murder, but he has designs on Molly, too. Sam lingers in this world to help and comfort her—a connection that touched a nerve in the hearts of audiences everywhere. "He's stuck, that's what it is. He's in between worlds," was Oda Mae's great revelation. "You know it happens sometimes that the spirit gets yanked out so fast that the essence still feels it has work to do here," explains the once-considered-a-charlatan psychic.

Sam finds Oda Mae in the middle of a séance as she's pretending to channel the dead. Then, for what very well may be the first time, she goes on to actually receive his messages from the beyond—and she listens. Sam forces (only in the way that a pestering, relentless spirit can) Oda Mae to contact Molly.

Isn't it heartwarming to feel the presence of loved ones even after they've passed—even more so to think that our lives remain so important to them that they'd move into the spirit world and *still* care so strongly for us? From the time that my father passed when I was four years old, I had the sense that there was a "man" in my bedroom wall. It wasn't until much later that I came to realize that this presence was actually my father—checking in on me and making sure I was okay.

In *Ghost,* Sam's afterlife presence is comforting to Molly, and as he watches her, his heart swells with love, realizing all he's left behind. In death, he's finally able to tell her he loves her.

In his review of the film in the *Chicago Sun-Times,* Roger Ebert had this to say: "The movie's single best scene—one that does touch the poignancy of the human belief in life after death—comes when Swayze is able to take over Goldberg's body, to use her physical presence as an instrument for caressing the woman that he loves."

Wait, what's that? A mainstream movie critic talking about massively spiritual and metaphysical concepts like life after death? Yes, Sam does inhabit Oda Mae's body, which, as Ebert also points out, should involve Moore and Goldberg in an intimate tango. But Zucker wisely chose to keep the scene in the "spiritual" realm, so we become lost in the poignancy of Sam and Molly's blissful reunion as the strains of the Righteous Brothers' "Unchained Melody" swells in the background. I'd be hard-pressed to believe that anyone had a dry eye when they saw *that.*

Another lasting and notable aspect of *Ghost* is how it differentiates between the afterlife experience for who we might call the "just" and "unjust." When Sam actually does move on at the end of the film, he's bathed in a beautiful white light, in total peace and happy expectation. However, when both Carl and the man he hired to kill Sam die in the film, frightening shadow figures emerge from beneath the streets to claim their souls. You see the terror in their faces, and it's obvious that they're not exactly being spirited away to heaven in a sea of brilliant light to meet the beaming faces of old friends and loved ones.

To some, this can be interpreted as both guys going to hell, and that, in my opinion, is the beauty of Spiritual

Cinema—that it leaves this interpretation up to the viewer. Zucker doesn't explain the scene or preach hellfire and brimstone; rather, he merely gives us one way of looking at how his characters move on. Nonetheless, the tortured spirits grabbing at Carl's heels and tugging him on give us an opportunity to reflect on our own interpretations of "hell." As Albert Lewis says in *What Dreams May Come,* "Hell is not always fire and brimstone. The real hell is your life gone wrong."

Could self-examination without the ability to rationalize be the worst hell? Imagine a soul who's come to life to learn specific lessons, but then goes far off that track. What worse pain could a soul imagine than knowing that it's actually *de*volved rather than *e*volved?

To paraphrase a wonderful line from Neil Simon's play *Chapter Two,* what if you'd gotten all the way to M and realized that you had to go back to A and start again? And what if you didn't have either the crutch of blame or the manipulation of self-pity at your disposal? Well, you'd just have to trudge back to the start of the line and begin again. That's a very powerful and important message as we try to negotiate the challenges of life—and *Ghost,* in all its beauty and reverence, reminds us all of the beauty of love . . . in life and beyond.

Groundhog Day
(February 2, 1993)

And now, as Monty Python would say, for something completely different. When *Groundhog Day* first came out, Gay was giving a talk at a large New Thought church in Portland, Oregon. As he remembers:

The minister, Reverend Mary Manin Morrissey, is a dear and longtime friend of mine. She and I were having coffee before my talk, and as almost always happens when we visit with each other, our conversation turned to movies. "Have you seen *Groundhog Day?*" she asked. I said I hadn't, and was somewhat surprised that she mentioned it, because I'd dismissed it as just another Bill Murray screwball comedy. "Go," she said. "Not only is it funny, it's one of the most spiritual films I've ever seen."

Now that was saying something, because Mary is one of the most spiritual people I know. I took her advice, and to this day it remains one of the most insightful movies I've had the pleasure to view.

Groundhog Day is a wonderful human story about being given the rare opportunity to live several lifetimes in one day. Packaged as a comedy to mainstream movie-goers, the underlying spiritual message is one that we, as seekers, have to do a little more work to find.

Harold Ramis's fantastic film is about learning the lessons we need in order to evolve in life and how the universe chooses to reveal those lessons to us. And it's a perfect example of the way a humorous film can advance spiritual messages couched in jokes and humor—it's a lot easier for an audience to suspend their disbelief when they know they're seeing a comedy. Since they aren't being asked to take anything seriously, what they get out of the film is up to them. And that's where *Groundhog Day* crosses the threshold into great Spiritual Cinema.

Phil Conner (Murray) is a cynical weatherman who is sent to Punxsutawney, Pennsylvania, to cover the annual appearance of their eponymous groundhog—an event Phil loathes. He's grumpy, sarcastic, and a punisher of equal opportunity to all around him, particularly Rita (Andie MacDowell), the segment producer on the shoot.

When a blizzard hits the dreary small town, Phil and crew are forced to stay the night. Waking the next morning to the sounds of Sonny and Cher's "I Got You Babe" on the clock radio, Phil discovers that it's Groundhog Day all over again. (By the way, the use of this tune, which many people consider one of the most annoying songs ever written, as a running theme in the movie is nothing short of inspired.) Everyone and everything stays the same, except for Phil. And it keeps happening, day after day after day. . . .

While Phil initially finds all this incredibly depressing, in time he comes to see it as the perfect opportunity to subtly seduce the lovely Rita. He learns more about her each day, and then uses what he's gleaned to try to impress her. And since each day is brand-new to Rita, with none of "yesterday's" experiences rolling over into the next, she's easily duped.

Phil tries his hand at piano—Rita loves men who play instruments—and works tirelessly to get her into bed. Ultimately, he comes to realizes that no "act" of kindness or chivalry will undo her Catholic-school training in just one day. He grows increasingly depressed, so much so that he tries to commit suicide, several times and in several ways. The only problem is that each morning, he keeps waking up at 6 A.M. to Sonny and Cher.

But what if there were *other* ways that Phil could use Groundhog Day to his advantage? What if each "new" day brought an opportunity that was more positive than throwing himself relentlessly at the reluctant Rita? What if he could actually use his experiences for good—that is, for someone other than himself? He knows everything that's going to happen in Punxsutawney on that particular day, so he could, for instance, always be under the right tree to catch a boy who falls out of it, or deftly perform the Heimlich maneuver on a choking diner at the perfect time.

The universe is presenting Phil with the same day, over and over again, until he masters it. His challenge is to grow less egocentric and learn to interact more positively with those around him, to be of service to the world.

After reliving this day hundreds, maybe even thousands, of times, our hero is finally at his newly evolved best, and that's when Rita falls in love with him. And when she goes to sleep in his arms, tomorrow is an actual new day—for the first time. In other words, the universe allows Phil to wake up with Rita on a different day, at a different time, as a changed man.

Groundhog Day is Murray at his comedic best. But what's ultimately at play is a much deeper, incredibly profound spiritual message: that the universe continues to teach us lessons until we learn them, from one lifetime to another, from one day to the next. In Phil, we see the evolution of an enlightened seeker: As he learns something new about himself each day, he uses it the next to help the world around him. So if *we* can learn and grow in each day, of each lifetime, then we can truly evolve into the people we were meant to be, too.

Forrest Gump
(July 6, 1994)

I don't think I've ever left a movie theater feeling better about being human than I did when I saw *Forrest Gump* for the first time back in 1994.

When a movie puts even one of its lines of dialogue into the public consciousness, it's quite a feat. I can think of a few films with famous one-liners, such as Clark Gable in *Gone with the Wind:* "Frankly, my dear, I don't give a damn"; Humphrey Bogart in *Casablanca:* "Here's looking at you, kid" and "This is the start of a beautiful friendship"; or Deborah Kerr in *An Affair to Remember:* "Winters must be cold for those with no warm memories."

Yet *Forrest Gump* has *several* of those endearing, time-tested, quotable lines that we'll all be saying for years to come, including "Like Mama always says, life is like a box of chocolates. You never know what you're gonna get" (speaking to the unpredictability of the world's uncertainties); "That's all I have to say about that" (on being resolute and making a point); "Stupid is as stupid does" (Forrest's mother's reminder that no one is *inherently* dumb); "I'm not a smart man, but I know what love is" (Forrest's final proclamation to the woman he loves); and, of course, "Run, Forrest, run!" (Jenny's solution to any troubles that may arise for him).

When a film penetrates our consciousness, is a huge box-office smash, and wins armloads of Academy Awards like *Forrest Gump,* something very powerful is at work.

I think that the opening credits—symbolically, metaphorically, and literally—capture all that is the life of Tom Hanks's earnestly charming titular character.

Director Robert Zemeckis, who later directed Hanks again in *Cast Away* and is very Spielberg-esque in his command of magically stunning special effects (see the *Back to the Future* trilogy, *Death Becomes Her*, and *Who Framed Roger Rabbit?*), opens the film by following the path of a small white feather. It's suspended in air, floating dreamily from one frame to the next, touching down at points and then spiriting away to higher grounds, breezily winding through the air as if on wings. That feather, and its seemingly circumstantial yet determined path, represents the charmed life of Forrest Gump.

Forrest, who seems to possess a somewhat "simple" intelligence, navigates life with the same luck and charm as that enchanted feather—simply "happening" upon some of the greatest and most significant cultural events of the latter half of the 20th century. "I don't know if we each have a destiny," Forrest wonders, "or if we're all just floatin' around accidental-like on a breeze." But, he wisely assures us, he thinks that it might be both. Yet no matter what, Forrest remains the same loving, unassuming boy from Greenbow, Alabama, who loves his mama (and chocolates).

The story opens with an adult Forrest waiting at a bus stop, sharing his life story with any and all who come to sit with him. Through flashbacks, we follow the magical trail of our floating feather as young Forrest inspires an as-yet-unknown Elvis Presley to adopt a jerky hip-thrusting dance move; as Forrest becomes an all-American football star and spends an afternoon in the White House; as Forrest meets three presidents (Kennedy, Johnson, and Nixon) and inspires John Lennon to write the famous song "Imagine"; as Forrest just "happens" to play a major role in the Vietnam War, the peace rallies in Washington, desegregation in the South, and Watergate.

He starts a shrimping business out of loyalty to one of his fallen Vietnam comrades, is on the only boat to survive a massive hurricane, becomes incredibly wealthy, and just "happens" to be one of the early investors in Apple computers, which he calls "some kind of fruit company." When a friend calls to explain that Forrest doesn't have to worry about money anymore, Forrest's take is, "That's good! One less thing."

Forrest Gump is grounded in the same theme as *Being There,* starring Peter Sellers as Chauncey Gardener: Life is a state of mind. But Chauncey had nothing on Forrest.

An innocent love and charming spirit buoys Forrest's soul and endears him to everyone he meets, mostly due to the unconditional love of his devoted mother (played by Sally Field). "Remember what I told you, Forrest," she says to her young son. "You're no different than anybody else is." She rallies tirelessly to allow Forrest a "normal" education, to let nothing stand in the way of his maturation and growth. Corrective leg braces weren't a handicap, but "special shoes," according to her, which will one day help her son fly. She sees the good in every situation, and encourages Forrest tirelessly to perform, achieve, and love.

It's this love that he shares with everyone he meets, particularly Jenny Curran (Robin Wright, before she added the "Penn"), the love of his life. Forrest meets Jenny on the bus on his first day of school when she invites him to sit next to her. He knows immediately that he's found a kindred spirit, and that's it for the rest of his life. No matter what Jenny says or does, Forrest never wavers in his feelings for her. As he says, "We were like peas and carrots, Jenny and I was."

Through all of his trials and tribulations, it's his love for Jenny that keeps him alive and literally strings the movie along. Some critics thought that the Jenny/Gump relationship was a nonsensical "thread," clumsily inserted into the plot to simply tie all of Forrest's epic adventures together. But for me, this enduring, endearing connection is more than just a plot device—it's the ultimate example of unconditional love, and the best illustration of this virtue in all of the Spiritual Cinema classics.

As peaceful and gentle as Forrest is, he attacks three different men whom he sees hurting Jenny. (He's right twice—once she was merely "entangled" in some heavy petting.) And he just continues to love her unconditionally. He writes her a letter every day from Vietnam, all of which go unanswered. Just when he thinks he's lost her forever, he takes the stage at an antiwar protest in Washington, D.C., and she jumps into the reflective pool and runs to him. Jenny, who's already abandoned Forrest several times—sometimes for other men—is about to take off again with one of the guys Forrest punched. As she's about to leave this time, she asks why he's so good to her. He answers, "Because you're my girl."

What a beautiful, uncomplicated, unselfish idea! Forrest's notion of love requires so little in return that he'll feel that way forever, even when Jenny gives him very little evidence to support his assumption that she's his girl. In fact, she continually abandons him for someone, or something, else. But it doesn't matter to Forrest. He absolutely loves Jenny, and nothing could ever change that—not her folk-singer dreams, her Black Panther days, or her drug-addled San Francisco wanderings. Talk about the power of a belief system! Forrest just *knows* that Jenny is his one true love, and that's all that matters to him.

When she does come to him after he's lost his mama and is living alone in his childhood home, he asks her to marry him. Although she never says no outright, Forrest knows her answer. Then, in one of the most touching, memorable exchanges of the entire film, he pleads, "Why don't you love me, Jenny? I'm not a smart man, but I know what love is."

Jenny does go on to get pregnant with their child (a very young Haley Joel Osment) and leaves again. When the film cuts back to present time, we realize that Forrest is waiting for a bus to so that he can meet his son. Then Jenny returns to Forrest one last time, with their son, to die. Again touching on one of the major (unfortunate) cultural milestones of the latter half of the 20th century, Jenny has AIDS—or, in her words, "a disease that the doctors don't know how to cure."

Now Forrest has a "smart" son to raise, and the film closes as Forrest, Jr., sets off for his first day of school. Forrest, Sr., bends down to the boy and starts, "Now don't . . ." but trails off. Was he about to impart that same knowledge that his mother so lovingly gave years ago, that he's no different from anyone else? Instead, he tells little Forrest that he loves him. And then a breeze picks up a small white feather. . . .

The clear message of *Forrest Gump* is the power of love and the title character's unwavering, unquestioning belief in it. No matter what, he loves purely and unconditionally, above all else.

And that's all I have to say about that.

The Matrix Trilogy**

The Matrix is a brilliantly conceived and executed metaphysical thriller/action movie that was offered as a trilogy, executed on a grand scale, and cost hundreds of millions of dollars. Here we're going to mainly consider the first and final entries in the series (*The Matrix* and *The Matrix Revolutions*) because these works contain the essence of the spiritual messages that the movies deliver.

On the surface, *The Matrix* is a fast-paced, visual-effects-laden movie with all the attending blood, gore, and suspense of a "mainstream" action flick. But underneath all that, a breathtaking metaphysical message unfolds that's almost unprecedented in big-budget Hollywood moviemaking.

The film asks viewers to accept the following: that the life they're living isn't real, that there is no objective reality, and that we live in a very complex experiment in which we're merely players. The core concept of *The Matrix* is that we're living in an elaborately constructed illusion—the kind of thinking that's at the very heart of metaphysics. The fact that it got expressed in a motion picture with fantastic critical and commercial success says a lot about where we are as a humanity at the turn of the century. But the fact that it got made with a major star (Keanu Reeves) from a major studio (Warner Bros.) says a lot about where mainstream filmmakers are at the turn of the century, too. We—both as a society and an industry—are signaling our readiness to explore our existence with open minds. We need to closely examine exactly how extraordinary its depiction in a mainstream film really is.

The spine of the story is the mystery surrounding what "the matrix" really is and why the powers that be are so determined to eradicate those who would dare to find it. Neo, Keanu Reeves's character, is in search of something that he can't identify. He doesn't know why he's so driven to find Morpheus (Laurence Fishburne), but he's utterly obsessed with the quest.

When the two finally meet, we learn from Morpheus that the matrix "is all around us, the wool that has been pulled over your eyes to blind you to the truth. You are living in a prison of your own mind. You can't be told what the matrix is—you must see it for yourself." A great many of us resonate with the wisdom of his observation.

The world that Neo thinks he's living in is not real. He thinks it's 1999, when it's actually at least 200 years later. In the interim, humanity has pioneered an advanced form of artificial intelligence that then "spawned" an entire race of machines that depended, they thought, on solar power to exist. Machines quickly began to take over the world, so humans "torched the sky" to cut off the machines' source of power. Undaunted, the machines found a way to take energy from human bodies and invented a new way to harvest their own beings.

As Morpheus explains to Neo: "The matrix is a computer-generated dream world built to keep us under control, so we can actually be an energy source to continue to power their machines."

When Neo is ultimately taken into the matrix, he finds that the life he was living was nothing more than an elaborately conceived program in a surreal world. The matrix is not the "real world"—the real world is something completely different. The only "real city" that appears to remain is (appropriately) Zion, near the core of the Earth.

Sentient machines seek out those who have discovered the secret and are looking for Zion. Prophesized by an oracle, Neo learns he's actually the reincarnation of the first man who began to discover the truth about the matrix. The remainder of the film revolves around Neo's slow realization that he is "the one" destined to save humanity.

On one level, this portends a dark, cataclysmic future engineered by a cruel hoax. But while it sounds nihilistic, the existence of "the matrix" questions the very nature of reality. That concept itself is at once both achingly beautiful and radical—a daring leap forward in the annals of moviemaking.

What is real? The critical message of the film is that we simply have no way of knowing. "Everything that has a beginning must have an end." Or does it?

The groundbreaking series (but not its impact) comes to a conclusion with *Matrix Revolutions,* which I believe will be remembered for decades to come as a seminal step forward in the potential of Spiritual Cinema. It does nothing less than remind us of the complex beauty and paradox of our humanity.

The symbolism (and fascination) of the film starts with the title itself: *Revolutions,* plural. This isn't just going to be the standoff between humanity and technology—the word's multiple meanings point to our evolving, and becoming a society where the ascension of racial equality and feminine energy has reached such an apogee that the heroes of the film are, save for Neo, women and people of color. With a nod to John Lennon, "imagine" that—it's not too hard if you just try.

The visuals in the trilogy are dazzling and majestic, but it's always been its philosophical and metaphysical musings that have made the series so extraordinary.

Revolutions illuminates both the challenges and breathtaking opportunities of humanity on the brink of knowing the unknowable. As is said in the film, "I didn't know . . . but I did believe." The film hints at the potential answers to our existence—including the human experiment, the "illusion" of life, and the ephemeral nature of our notions of reality—it tantalizes, yet never so obviously robs us of our individual right to find the answers ourselves.

Challenges to us as an audience abound in *Revolutions,* not in plot "turnings," but rather in the fascinating ambiguities of the tantalizing clues that lead Neo and Trinity (Carrie-Anne Moss) to their destinies. We could discuss this for hours and hours—and will as the years unfold—but space here allows us only to examine one of the film's most exhilarating complexities.

The crux of Neo's journey in *Revolutions* is explained early on by the Oracle, who tells him, "No one can see beyond a choice that they don't understand." *Choice*—the word and concept behind it lie at the center of *The Matrix,* but they've also become perhaps one of the key concepts of our evolving humanity. We've chosen a path of destruction before in Atlantean, Mayan, and Egyptian societies. One of the crucial tenets of the new spirituality of the last half century has been our recognition that fate is not indeed thrust upon us—we have choices.

Opportunity can present itself, yes, but our fate is never forced upon us as inevitable. In other words, we can choose to hear the clarion cry of our soul's call to adventure or ignore it altogether. *We* have the final say as to whether or not we'll actually move into that eternal flow of our own destiny. If we do make that leap, we almost immediately sense at the core of our beings that the choice has been made from a deep well within our own heart and consciousness, yet it remains just beyond our ability to totally comprehend. Nevertheless, we're forevermore drawn forward by the choice we've made to engage the world of mystery and paradox.

Getting back to the movie, Neo and Trinity have a passionate love for each other, but both have a knowing on a deep soul level that they must choose to push inexorably forward, regardless of the consequences, at each moment. As one character notes early on about them: "Remarkable how close the pattern of love is to the pattern of insanity."

Neo comments much later in the film that he persists in his quest simply because he chooses to do so. If for no other reason than the spotlight the film focuses on our freedom (and responsibility) to choose—including the right to pick conception, birth, freedom, and reality itself—*Revolutions* deserves our attention and respect.

And they saved the best for last. Not since *2001: A Space Odyssey* has there been a more intricate and fascinating closing ten minutes than in *Revolutions*. I believe that film classes will be discussing this ending for years to come, and the interpretations will be as varied as they were for Kubrick's film. The Wachowski brothers, who conceived, wrote, and directed the trilogy, won't discuss their interpretation of the ending of the series—they respect our right to choose, and somewhere, Kubrick must be smiling.

However, the brothers have been faulted recently for making concessions to commerciality: $300 million to make the last two movies in the series created a daunting balancing act, but I personally believe that the filmmakers deserve our awe and respect as true visionaries who have introduced concepts into mainstream culture.

Remember the marketing campaign for the first *Matrix*—was there even an indication of this core concept? Not at all. It was a cool-looking summer movie, right? Now, it wasn't misrepresented in its marketing or a victim of false advertising—it was just incomplete. The movie was sold for what the surface story was, and that worked. I know from my own discussions with some of those involved in the process that the studio executives didn't focus on the underlying message of the film at all.

The Wachowskis were brilliant in the way the constructed the project, because it obviously worked on an experiential, visceral level as an action film, and that's how the studio chose to market it. In many ways it *is* a very traditional, violent action movie with extraordinary visual effects. (The same company that pioneered the painted-world sections of *What Dreams May Come*—Mass Illusions/Manex—created the effects for *The Matrix* and deservedly won Academy Awards for their efforts on both.)

The underlying spiritual message was left for the audiences to discover, and that's great. The movie got made, and the message is there: Reality is subjective rather than objective.

At some time in the future, the movie industry will catch up to both the world culture and their publishing/music counterparts, and then these movies will be identified for what they are: Spiritual Cinema. For now, it's terrific that *The Matrix Trilogy* made it through the process so well.

The Sixth Sense **

(August 6, 1999)

Cole Sear (Haley Joel Osment) is haunted by dead people. They chase him down streets, surprise him in the corridors of his school, and wake him up in the middle of the night. Unfortunately, these aren't sweet spirits like Sam Wheat in *Ghost;* rather, these deceased individuals appear to Cole in all their gruesome and bloody glory. It's not until the boy meets child psychologist Malcolm Crowe (Bruce Willis) that he can make peace with his "visitors." Through Malcolm, Cole realizes that he actually has a special gift, one that he can use to help spirits who need to be seen.

The Sixth Sense is a moving reminder that spirits need not frighten us, and that they often require our help to transcend this plane. In fact, this film is one of the most brilliantly conceived and executed commercial vehicles for the continuum of life that I've ever seen. Through the Malcolm Crowe character, we see the gray area that exists between the states of life and death—and discover that there might not be all that much difference between them.

The film opens as Malcolm and his wife, Anna, celebrate an award he received for his achievement in the field of child psychology, bestowed upon him by the city of Philadelphia. They playfully retreat to their bedroom but are greeted by a broken window and dead phone lines. A grotesque, skeletal intruder stands naked in their bathroom—we find out that it's Vincent Gray, a former patient who's now paying a visit to the doctor who couldn't help him. Vincent fires his gun at Malcolm and then turns the weapon on himself.

The scene ends, and we next see Dr. Crowe studying a legal pad on an outdoor bench. As he endeavors to unearth the mystery that cursed his troubled avenger, he meets nine-year-old Cole along the way. They first meet in a church, where Cole plays earnestly with a handful of toy soldiers, whispering a phrase in Latin: *"De profundis clamo ad te domine."* A translation of this harrowing phrase reveals that Cole is far from your average imaginary-soldier-playing kid: "Out of the depths, I cry to you, oh Lord."

The Sixth Sense benefits from a magnificent plot twist, which is that Malcolm Crowe died the night he was shot by Vincent Gray. The thing is, Malcolm doesn't know that he's dead. But the film is not without its share of subtle hints—for example, the dinner table in Malcolm's home has a place setting for just one (his wife). And when he shows up late to eat with her and apologizes, she doesn't even look up. Instead, she slips out of the restaurant without ever acknowledging him, whispering only "Happy anniversary" to some fixed point in the distance.

Malcolm can't open doors, he's rarely seen having a reciprocal conversation with anyone other than Cole, and he combs the streets of Philadelphia in the same grayish-blue shirt and drab olive overcoat day after day, yet never once does he realize that he's dead. This brilliant plot device is revealed only minutes before the film's conclusion and came to most viewers as quite a surprise. That death can be a gray area, one that feels and looks like life, should give us all reason to believe.

Cole has quite a different relationship with death. His house is always cold, for instance, and an ethereal glow frames his face in every photo hung on the walls of his home. He opens drawers in his kitchen without moving a muscle. He inexplicably knows the adolescent nickname of his teacher and that people were hung on the school's grounds hundreds of years before when it was a courthouse. His mother's beloved bumblebee pendant, which once belonged to Cole's grandmother, keeps moving from his mother's closet into his bureau drawer. He has a gift, but he thinks that even Dr. Crowe won't be able to help him. "I don't want to be scared anymore," he says.

After a band of mischievous classmates sends Cole to the hospital, Malcolm Crowe comes for a visit. Cole, piping up from his hospital bed, decides to tell him what's really going on. "I want to tell you my secret now," he says. "I see dead people." Cole sees them walking around like "regular" people—and (which Malcolm will come to reflect upon later when he finally realizes that he's dead), "They don't see each other; they only see what they want to see. They don't know that they're dead." And that, most chillingly, "they're everywhere."

Of course we know that Malcolm himself is among this cadre of haunted visages. But when he steps outside the hospital to record Cole's diagnosis into a pocket tape recorder ("visual hallucinations, paranoia, schizophrenia"), we see that he still hasn't come around. Until he can believe Cole, Malcolm will continue to languish between the world of the living and dead, frustrated, unheard, and unable to communicate with his wife. As we're journeying along with him, trying to understand the continuum of life, we want to believe little Cole and feel the truth of his uncomfortable visions. (Genius, again, on the part of writer/director M. Night Shyamalan to take us on this journey through the eyes of an innocent boy. I share with others the belief that babies and young children all have a very strong connection to who they really are, as well as the worlds between lives; we understand that children know something really special.)

When Malcolm thinks that he's reached the end of his rope—that his family is falling apart because his wife won't speak to him—he tries to release Cole from his care. He tells the boy that he can't treat him anymore, but he'll transfer him to another doctor. Cole, convinced that Malcolm is the only one who can help him, asks through his tears, "You believe me, right? Dr. Crowe, you believe my secret, right?"

Using his typical restraint, the good doctor replies, "I don't know how to answer that, Cole."

"How can you help me if you don't believe me?" the boy counters.

Rather than abandoning his tortured patient, Malcolm goes back to the drawing board. He delves deeper into the history of former patient Vincent Gray, convinced that the two boys share a common affliction—what, he doesn't know. Malcolm pores over textbooks, flips through old legal pads, and scrutinizes hours of tape, when he makes a startling discovery on the recording of a session with Vincent. As Malcolm listens intently to the tape, he hears his secretary interrupting the session, saying that he's needed on the phone.

"Vincent," he says, "I have to take this. Give me a minute," and footsteps on the tape indicate that he's left the room. In the empty space that fills the dead air (pun intended), Malcolm hears a faint scuffle that gives him pause. The tape continues to play, and by the time Malcolm has returned to his patient, Vincent is crying.

The doctor rewinds the tape, turns up the volume, and clearly hears a terrified voice pleading in Spanish while he's out of the room: *"Yo no quiero morir . . . sálvame . . . sálvame."* ("I don't want to die, save me, save me.") This, we realize, is what Vincent saw. The proverbial light bulb goes off in Malcolm's head, and he gets it: Vincent saw dead people. Now Malcolm has the proof he needs to believe that Cole does, too.

By the time he meets with the boy again, Malcolm has figured out a way to make his ghosts disappear. He urges Cole to think about why the ghosts come to him. "They need help, even the scary ones," he responds. So the two determine that Cole can make his ghosts go away by just listening to them.

Later, when a young girl appears under Cole's home-made tent, he shudders but doesn't run. Kyra (played by a young Mischa Barton, whom many of you now know as the ingénue on *The O.C.* television series) vomits repeatedly, but then looks up and says hopefully, "I'm feeling much better now." Cole, visibly shaking, asks, "Do you want to tell me something?"

The next scene cuts to a brave Cole, riding a near-empty bus to the outskirts of the city. He's going to the little girl's wake so that he can uncover exactly what she was trying to communicate. He wades through the throngs of drab mourners (and the girl's mother in a shocking suit of red), and is drawn upstairs to Kyra's old bedroom. He surveys her discarded dolls and her hospital-like bed—the cold sterility of what should have been a room vibrating with young life.

The camera cuts quickly to the trembling, pale girl, cowering under her bed and eyeing Cole. She pushes a videotape across the floor, and without missing a beat, he delivers the tape directly to her father and leaves the wake. When Dad pops the tape into the VCR, he finds a hidden camera capturing his wife pouring Pine-Sol into their daughter's soup.

Cole's work here is done.

Later, the boy gifts his harried doctor with the one thing he needs to know: how to communicate with his wife. "Wait until she's asleep," he casually advises. "She'll listen to you, and she won't even know it." Cole is so beyond his years that he knows how to do what even a grown man can't. And Osment delivers a believable, heart-wrenching performance of a troubled young boy who, when all is said and done, is just a kid.

When Malcolm comes home that night, he finds his beautiful Anna asleep in front of the TV, playing their wedding video as she does every night. A chill comes over the room, and her breath forms a cloud as she asks, "Why did you leave me?" Confused, Malcolm replies that he didn't.

As his wedding ring rolls onto the ground, Malcolm suddenly realizes that he hadn't been wearing it, and Cole's voice comes to him: "I see people—they don't know they're dead." Malcolm stumbles back through the house. He again sees the table setting for one, flashes back to Anna's solo anniversary dinner, and remembers a table stacked against the cellar door to his office. He sees her cold breath and hears Vincent's gunshot again, and then Dr. Crowe, stunned, stops mid-step and feels his stomach—and sees the bloodstain on the back of his shirt.

"I think I can go now," he tells his sleeping wife, at once understanding what this journey has been about. He just had to help someone, and he thinks he did. "And I needed to tell you something," he says. "You were never second, ever. I love you."

She winces visibly at the admission, and he assures her that everything will be different in the morning. He says good night and closes his eyes in resignation. A brilliant white light fills the screen and fades to their kiss on the wedding video. Malcolm Crowe's heaven is that happy day with his wife. And now he's found it.

Whale Rider
(January 18, 2003)

When an old paradigm dies, a magical opportunity is born. In the suspended moment in time before the new one takes shape, the space between solution and resolution presents powerful transcendence to those who feel their hearts pulled to the call. Pai, the 13-year-old heroine of *Whale Rider,* hears the call of ancient whales drawing her to her destiny. It is this destiny that challenges and ultimately dismantles the long-held Maori tradition of leadership that she's been steeped in.

Whale Rider is set in New Zealand, where the Maori people claim descent from Paikea, named "Whale Rider" for his epic journey on the back of such a creature after a capsized canoe threatened to take his life. For the next 1,000 years, Paikea's legacy has ensured a male heir for the title of chief. But when the current chief's eldest son, Porourangi, has twins—a boy and a girl—and both mother and son die in childbirth, the tribe faces extinction when only the girl survives. Wracked with grief, Porourangi disappears, breaking the traditional line of succession. The time for a new paradigm, like it or not, is upon the Maori people.

Pai (Keisha Castle-Hughes) is left to live with her grandparents and wants desperately to be acknowledged by them. Koro, the grandfather and tribal leader, harbors a deep sadness and sense of loss both for his son, who has disappeared, and his deceased grandson. Even though little Pai has been given the name of the ancient founder of the tribe, Koro can't for a moment believe that she's the one destined to lead them. She is, after all, "just a girl," and the lineage of the tribe clearly requires a firstborn *male* heir.

Change is but a distant ray of sun on the faraway horizon, but Pai is drawn to its light, undaunted by her embittered grandfather and the restrictions her culture places on women. In one of the most heart-wrenching scenes in the film, Pai prepares to sing a traditional Maori chant at the school talent show. The night of the show, she gazes longingly into an audience of parents, searching for her beloved grandfather in the sea of faces. She bravely steps center stage and dedicates her performance to him. Her tiny voice fills the room, wavering as she realizes that he's chosen not to be there. We want so badly for him to appear and witness her heartfelt performance and recognize the respect she has for the ancient traditions of her people. Undeterred by her grandfather's absence, Little Pai sings on, bravely holding back tears.

Meanwhile, Koro is more convinced than ever that the tribe must secure an heir to the throne. He calls for the boys from the village, and starts an exclusive training school for them where he hopes that through grueling training exercises and practice, the natural leader of the tribe will emerge. The boys, however, have little respect for the primitive battle techniques and ancient tribal chants, preferring their boom boxes and Game Boys over tradition. Pai hides furtively beneath the windows and lurks in the shadows so that she, too, can take in her grandfather's revered wisdom, which is forbidden to her.

From a Western perspective, it's difficult to watch this culture suppress and deny the potential of women. We've enjoyed films such as *The Hours* and *Far from Heaven* (both of which are explored in the next chapter) that capture the emergence and ascension of feminine energy in our society—but *Whale Rider* is set in the present day, where

Maori women are still unable to ride in a canoe, fight, or participate in certain tribal incantations. Pai, ever the fearless visionary, continues to follow her heart without a sense of anger or rebellion. She's possessed by the clarity of sight singular to mapmakers who have chosen to answer their destiny, regardless of consequence.

Meanwhile, deep within the ocean, a massive herd of whales is drawn toward the shores of Pai's village. In breathtaking and achingly real cinematography, the giant creatures eventually land on the beach, where they're stranded and sure to die. Nowhere is the symbolic alignment of man and animal more prevalent—the whales' tortured cries echo the pain and anguish of little Pai, who's been ignored and dismissed by her grandfather and her tribe.

Pai's moment of grace and opportunity arrives in this metaphoric crisis. Her grandfather is certain that the whales' destiny signals the death of the Maori tribe. As their cries draw her to the restless shore, Pai's heart is deeply conflicted with her love for her grandfather and his respect for tradition, but she can't deny the call to change her tribe's future. She's certain that she can save the whales and her tribe. First, however, she must confront her grandfather, which she does, tearfully and boldly.

The community bands together to push the whales back out to sea, led by Pai—the newly emergent leader of their broken tribe—who shines as the one destined to guide her people. Castle-Hughes's performance was beyond Oscar-worthy; her nomination for Best Actress of 2003 was more than earned.

Pai's bold vision illuminates the existence of fate and the certainty of destiny in a story that is the very soul of Spiritual Cinema. This film bathes us in light and fills our hearts with the purity of its essence, of

Pai's strength of character, and of the Maori existence and harmony with nature. This courageous story awakens our consciousness to the powerful possibilities of transcendence, magical opportunity, and challenging and dismantling outdated belief systems. With the existence of films like *Whale Rider,* we can be certain that the world is collectively extending its arms to greet the approaching dawn of a new paradigm.

Eternal Sunshine of the Spotless Mind**

(March 19, 2004)

Like the siren call of *Eternal Sunshine of the Spotless Mind's* theme song (which is performed by Beck in the opening and closing credits), this movie encourages us to change our hearts and look around us.

Now, imagine that your heart has been broken. You were in love, but the relationship has ended badly. Then someone offers you the chance to erase that relationship, that person, and everything about it and them from your memory forever.

Would you do it?

Should you do it?

Could you do it?

Such is the provocative premise of *Eternal Sunshine of the Spotless Mind.* As with most films written by the brilliant Charlie Kaufman *(Adaptation* and *Being John Malkovich)*, the nonlinear plot of this movie makes it somewhat difficult to summarize. But it makes us talk, it makes us think, and it makes us wonder. . . . The complicated, clever charm of this brilliant production combines so many important characteristics of Spiritual Cinema—love, memory, consciousness, the illusion of time, the paths of our souls, and the "problems" of science—that it's an amalgamation of all the genre's classics that we've seen and loved until now, and makes a fitting end to our chapter.

The heart of the film takes place in the mind of its protagonist, Joel, played with nuance, sensitivity, and endearing vulnerability by Jim Carrey. (This is also the first role in which I believe that he just disappears into his character.) Clementine (played with heartbreaking, poignant, eclectic, and luminescent beauty by the inestimable Kate Winslet) and Joel find a blissful love that is reflected both in their differences (his shyness and her extroverted charm) and their similarities (a mutual love of Chinese food and sharing adventures at night in the dark). Unfortunately, they repeat patterns from previous relationships, which ultimately leads to their separation. On a whim, Clem decides to have Joel erased from her memory after the relationship ends on a sour note. When Joel finds out, he has her erased, too.

As Joel remembers Clementine, the great love of his life, each memory is, at his request, systematically erased. In an amusing exchange in the shabby-looking offices of Lacuna, Inc., Joel asks Dr. Howard Mierzwiak (Tom Wilkinson) if there's "any risk of brain damage."

"Well," answers the doctor, "technically speaking, the operation *is* brain damage, but on a par with a night of heavy drinking. Nothing you'll miss." (That explains where some of *my* memories have gone! I *am* a "child" of the '70s, after all. . . .)

The film follows Joel's memories back in time as each one of Clem is erased, until they both realize that they don't want to lose each other and want the procedure to stop. In fact, the film opens as Joel has an inexplicable urge to ditch work and take a train to Montauk, New York. Why? It's on this train that he meets Clementine, seemingly for the first time, and they both experience a vague sense of familiarity—almost as if they already know each other.

Their great love, so it seems, has outdone the efforts of science. Clem and Joel aren't supposed to remember, let alone want to be with, one another—after all, they scientifically removed each other! Yet they're drawn to be together, and that's when we understand the true power of what they were trying to undo.

Can you erase someone you were meant to be with? Can you consciously buck the winds of your fate and redesign your future? Clem and Joel's determination to find one another and remain fixed in each other's memory offers a message of extraordinary promise. Perhaps, once and for all, they can shatter their negative relationship patterns and learn to be together in the way they were meant to be. The experiences of these two people seem to me to be a metaphor for that inexorable and evolutionary quest of our souls from lifetime to lifetime . . . and beyond. It's a tantalizing possibility that overrides the mechanics of science (and Dr. Howard's procedure). You simply cannot erase what's meant to be.

While surely a neurosurgeon or psychiatrist may have a different, more "technical," explanation for Joel and Clem's unexpected reunion, my answer is this: Our memories in our waking, breathing existence make up one representation of our "reality," yet there are other states of our being that don't relate to our *waking* life, but rather belong to that infinite world of the *perpetual* life of our souls. A soul, and its multi-lifetime trajectory, is something that even science can't erase.

Within our soul groups, we journey from lifetime to lifetime with those to whom we've made an eternal commitment to pursue growth and evolution. When we meet someone in one lifetime, we may not "remember" them in a conscious sense, but a stored genetic memory of their essence triggers a memory—a familiarity that's as palpable and real, if not more so, as our five physical senses. We resonate in their presence as if we "know" them—because, in fact, we do.

The attraction that we feel may have no precedent in our conscious lives, but we nevertheless instinctively know each other. Even if that experience eventually becomes one of pain and sadness, we internally understand that our sacred pact of mutual growth has been honored. With this vision of consciousness, there are no victims or blame; instead, there are only commitments kept and promises fulfilled.

Isn't this all a metaphor for the journey through our lifetimes, when we make decisions in the world between death and life and then play out those commitments in the moments between life and death? How about when, no matter what, we recognize each other without the assistance of conscious memory—when we know that we've been together before (because we have)? Or when only the illusionary veil of the cycle of death and life separates us from remembering who we've been through each of the centuries?

When we make these eternal commitments, we have intentions that may not ever consciously occur to our human selves—but, somehow, some way, we find each other and play out the scenarios on our way home . . . to oneness.

Perhaps, then, at the depth and breadth of its vision, this amazing movie presents us with the hope that our running can finally come to an end in the *Eternal Sunshine of [Our] Spotless Mind*. As such, the film is nothing less than a reflection of those extraordinary promises that we make to each other, including the "knowing" that no disappointment or heartbreak can erase the blueprints of our souls, and that what is meant to be, will be. When entertainment accomplishes something like this, it transcends the experience of movies and touches the face of eternity . . . and offers tantalizing glimpses of who we may *really* be.

Chapter Three

THE NEW WAVE OF SPIRITUAL CINEMA:
Must-See Movies That Illuminate Facets of the Spiritual Landscape

In spite of declining ticket sales, mainstream Hollywood continues to go down the path of blockbuster action movies, a trend that a studio-executive friend of ours calls "pumping the popcorn machine." Meanwhile, in recent years there's been a much quieter but hopeful trend toward more spiritually satisfying movies, which are being made by filmmakers in- and out-side of the mainstream. We've been pleased—and pleas-antly surprised—by the growing number of heart-and-soul features that have appeared over the last few years. In this chapter we explore, salute, and encourage you to watch the best of the newer movies in the genre of Spiritual Cinema.

Again, please note that all films marked with two as-terisks (**) denote a description where Stephen discusses an important plot point that may "give away" some major plot revelations.

Cast Away**
(December 22, 2000)

We begin this chapter with a film that contains one of the great performances in cinematic history, all the more compelling because for half the movie, the main character is the only one onscreen. Beyond the remarkable acting, though, there are myriad treasures to be mined in this modern masterpiece.

Let's start by contemplating this question: What if we have more than just one soul mate? Could we find that one great love *more* than once?

Tom Hanks knows—he's answered the question twice, first in *Sleepless in Seattle* as a widower who finds love atop the Empire State Building, and then as a desert-island castaway whom fate redirects. Hanks is, in my opinion, the quintessential American hero, so why shouldn't he be in two seminal films that have shifted the public's consciousness of love? If this talented actor had been around a few decades ago, couldn't you just imagine him in *It's A Wonderful Life* or *Harvey* or *Mr. Smith Goes to Washington?* And if their time on this planet had been reversed, wouldn't James Stewart have been perfect in *Forrest Gump* or *Cast Away?*

Getting back to the movie at hand, in *Cast Away,* Hanks plays globe-trotting FedEx systems analyst Chuck Noland, who has found his soul mate in fiancée Kelly (Helen Hunt). Just as he leaves for another company trip, she gives him a pocket watch with her picture in it—unfortunately, the plane he's in crashes, and he winds up alone on a tropical island for four years.

While on the island, Chuck's devotion to Kelly is what keeps him going. When he finally escapes and returns to claim his lost love, he's left to discover that she's married someone else. The reunion scene between the two lovers is wrenchingly beautiful and haunting because Chuck realizes that Kelly had to accept his death and move on. Even though she acknowledges that he's the love of her life, she's made a new commitment to her husband and young daughter. Both Chuck and Kelly are left with the painful realization that she can't return to him and what they once had.

So what is he to do? Has he really lost his soul mate? For the moment, he has. But maybe, just maybe, there is someone else. . . .

In the very beginning of the film, a FedEx truck makes a pickup from a sculptor at an isolated home somewhere in America. We follow her package to Moscow, where Chuck also just "happens" to be. When his plane crashes, Chuck is washed up on the island with a lot of packages, all of which he ultimately opens—except for one, which sports the distinct winglike logo of that sculptor. Without consciously knowing why, he keeps that package intact, and when he does escape, he not only takes it with him, but also paints the sender's logo on his sail.

After Chuck's ill-fated reunion with Kelly, he has a beautiful moment with a close friend, where he talks about life without Kelly, how his love for her kept him alive while he was stranded on the island, and about his botched suicide attempt. After Chuck failed in killing himself, he realized that he just had to keep going. Even though he was never logically convinced that he'd escape from the island, one day the tide washed up a large piece of hard plastic, which he was able to fashion into a sail, and he escaped. "So I know what I have to do now," he says to his friend of life without Kelly. "I gotta keep breathing, because tomorrow the sun will rise. Who knows what the tide will bring in?"

This optimism is an eloquent message of hope. And the time has come for all of us to leap into the unknown and trust that both the power of love—and the love of the universe—will guide us.

The universe decides that it's time for Chuck to deliver the package that he's protected for so long. After discovering that the sender isn't home, he leaves the box at the door with a note saying that it saved his life. Out on the highway again, he stops to decide which way to go, when a beautiful and charismatic woman in a pickup stops to help him. As she drives off, we note the winglike logo on the back of her truck. It's Bettina, the sculptor from the movie's first scene (played by the luminescent Lari White), and we see in Hanks's eyes that he's found his new direction.

The power of love is sometimes disguised in experiences we don't know how to interpret until we've lived them. The underlying hope of this film (and *Sleepless in Seattle*) is that we may indeed have more than one soul mate in life. True love, like lightning, *can* strike more than once. And for all of us who have loved and lost, that's a powerful and comforting message indeed.

The Family Man
(December 22, 2000)

Here's a film that truly has a hold on the challenges of modern times. Released in late 2000, *The Family Man* captures the complexities of having a career and family amid the fast-paced, demanding world of the 21st century, but it also challenges us to look at this juggling act with different eyes. How important *is* that business meeting if you have to miss an open house at your kid's school? Is the high-stakes world of success more important than true love? Can you balance love, family, and career so that no one, including you, feels cheated?

Many people have made choices in the last few decades to forego having families to focus on their careers. This is a very recent phenomenon—until the sexual revolution of the '60s and '70s, men didn't have to forego anything. They just pursued their careers and basically left the raising of children to their wives. The revolution changed all that when women, quite rightfully, said, "Hey, we deserve and demand our own identities, too." So "DINKS" (Double Income, No Kids) came into being, with the man *and* woman both pursuing professional lives. And nowadays, couples who do have children try valiantly to find the right balance. Even more extreme are the individuals who forget about relationships altogether as they focus on their work.

Children live in very different climates today than they did when traditional nuclear families were the norm 40 or 50 years ago. In fact, this societal upheaval in traditional roles, and the place of love in modern society, just might be the single biggest cultural challenge for humans today. We know that we can't go back to the way it was (and most of us don't want to), but we haven't quite figured out how to balance all of our needs and desires. And that begs the question: What are our priorities?

In *The Family Man,* Jack Campbell (Nicolas Cage) kisses his girlfriend, Kate Reynolds (Téa Leoni), goodbye after they graduate from college. He's about to head to London for a year of work—she begs him to stay, but he promises that he'll come back to her. He never does.

Twelve years later, Jack is a wealthy, successful president of an investment house living in a New York City high-rise. He sleeps with women whose name he either forgets or never asks, and he drives a Ferrari. So when he gets an unexpected call from his old love just before Christmas, he ignores it . . . marking the beginning of the end for "King of the Universe" Jack Campbell.

Shortly thereafter, he stumbles upon what appears to be an attempted robbery in a convenience store. Trying to thwart the "crime," Jack makes a deal with the thief, whose name is Cash (Don Cheadle), and tries to convince him to seek help. Cash gives Jack a mischievous look—what would make this guy think that he has it so much better than this stranger does? Cash reminds him that his life may not be as perfect as he thinks it is, and he warns Jack to remember that "you brought this on yourself."

The next morning, Jack wakes up in bed with Kate in New Jersey. They have two kids and a dog, and he works selling tires "retail!" for his father-in-law. He races to Manhattan to find that his old life there never happened. He meets Cash again, who tells him that Jack is getting a glimpse of the life he might have had. He leaves Jack to deal with the ramifications of the decision he made 12 years before.

Jack then discovers what his life would have been like if he'd stayed and married Kate: a dead-end job, a modest house in Jersey, no money (Kate's promising law career turned into pro bono work), and two kids with whom he has no idea how to interact. But Jack slowly learns more about them and grows from horrified to smitten. It is with Kate, however, that he discovers what he truly lost. He becomes aware of how much he once loved her, and that he never really stopped.

Just as he begins to realize that his love for Kate and their kids is more fulfilling than his old obsession with another kind of success, he wakes up again in his old life. And try as he might, he can't go back. He seeks Kate out and finds that not only has she become a successful lawyer, but she's also moving to Paris to head her firm there. He follows her to the airport and, in a lovely, romantic scene, tells her about the glimpse he had of who and what they could have been. He apologizes for having been so wrong and, in an ironic reversal, begs *her* not to go.

The Family Man's message of the power and preeminence of love couldn't come at a better time. When a film can entertain us, stir our hearts, and gently empower us to reexamine our priorities at the same time, then it is the absolute highest possible use of the art form we call cinema.

Mulholland Drive **

(October 8, 2001)

Within a three-month period in 2001, four break-out films came into the world that challenged the very nature of reality. *Mulholland Drive, A Beautiful Mind, Waking Life,* and *Vanilla Sky* were all released within a 90-day time frame. To paraphrase Shakespeare, something wonderful this way came, and we can very happily note that the questioning of reality itself has reached critical mass.

I'm fairly confident that anyone's take on what "really" happens in *Mulholland Drive* is somewhat beside the point. In fact, experiencing this movie is about surrendering, the letting go of our need for everything to make logical sense in the first moment we encounter it. This film confused some people and angered others, and everyone tended to either love it or hate it. When a work this polemic hurtles into public consciousness, it's an example of extraordinary filmmaking for me—after all, innovative movies *should* elicit a strong emotion. And it shouldn't come as any great surprise that something this daring and unique should come from David Lynch.

From his shocking version of *The Elephant Man* to the bravura creepiness of his short-lived early-'90s television series, *Twin Peaks,* Lynch has forged a totally unique identity. His movies are always triumphs of style, mood, and attitude; and he's maintained a "cult" following for creating abstract works of cinema. Much like life itself, his plots are never as important as the *experience.* (After all, to paraphrase a classic line in an REM song, life's about the journey, not the destination.) So when Lynch focuses his prodigious talent on a film about the entire experience of life and death, the result is mesmerizing, shocking, and exhilarating.

A young woman (Laura Elena Harring) seemingly escapes murder, only to endure a horrible car accident on Los Angeles's storied Mulholland Drive. "Mulholland," as it's known in L.A., sits at the very top of the Santa Monica Mountains that separate the San Fernando Valley from the rest of Los Angeles. It's a winding, twisting road that provides spectacular visual vistas, but it's also very dangerous, with several blind turns and no predictability—so it's the utterly perfect metaphor for the film.

The young woman crawls away from the crash unharmed, but she remembers nothing, least of all her own name. She hides away in a seemingly empty apartment, where she later meets young, bright-eyed, aspiring actress Betty Elms (Naomi Watts). Together, the two try to uncover her forgotten identity in the beguiling City of Angels. Or at least they seem to. For the rest of the movie, we're reminded of how the Beatles told us that nothing is real—or is it? (Some people also believe that the story is actually told in reverse—or is it?)

Along the way, the two women encounter a typically Lynchian landscape, which includes offbeat characters and casting (such as '40s dance goddess Ann Miller as a Hollywood landlady); a look at the experience of idealistic young people in the film business (both sympathetic and scathing); a Spanish-language performance of Roy Orbison's classic "Crying" that you will never forget; and some violence and steamy sex.

To his everlasting credit, Lynch won't reveal his own take on the underlying context of the film. But to me it seems that the entirety of the experience has happened in Betty's mind at the actual instant of her death. She confuses herself with her lover and best friend, and she remembers her life and the events that led to her death in a very subjective fashion (just as all reports of this experience indicate). Lynch has made an entire movie that's devoted to our experience in the last moments of our life, wherein we relive much of it in a nonlinear instant!

Lynch was nominated for an Academy Award for his direction. That the notoriously conservative Academy of Motion Pictures Arts and Sciences would honor a filmmaker such as this is a real testament to the bravura nature of Lynch's work. Mainstream recognition of his achievement is as surprising as it is delightful, as interest in metaphysical movies has not only achieved, but actually exceeded, critical mass. And for those of us who love films with these themes, that's great cause for celebration.

Waking Life
(October 19, 2001)

If the rallying cry of the '60s was to "question authority," then in this first decade of the new millennium, it must have evolved into "question reality." Movies are reflecting that fascination back to us in an astonishing way. *Waking Life,* for example, is a breathtaking and utterly metaphysical inquiry into a core question of spirituality and consciousness: What is more "real," what happens when we're awake or what happens when we're dreaming?

Compared to the other "breakout" metaphysical films of 2001, *Waking Life* is the one that got the least attention. In the fall of 2001, it was released in just a few art theaters and then—despite brilliant, glowing reviews from substantial critics such as Roger Ebert—it disappeared rather quickly into the world of DVD and video. Yet even though most of the world missed this film, I hope and believe that it will find an audience.

Director Richard Linklater *(Before Sunrise, Dazed and Confused, Before Sunset)* actually shot the footage in live action and then laid animation on top, creating an eerie, surreal look and feel to every frame. It creates an almost hypnotic atmosphere for the action of the film, which, truth be told, is nothing less than a psychological/spiritual/ metaphysical inquiry into the meaning and reality of life itself.

There truly is no story, per se—in fact, an analysis of *Waking Life* can't even be attempted in conventional terms. The film opens with a young girl telling a boy that "dream is destiny," and the rest of the movie plays out on that theme. The boy dreams that he's floating out into the ethers, and the rest of the picture explores his various waking and dream states, leaving the audience to continually wonder which is which. Along the way, he encounters a variety of philosophers, teachers, bartenders, street gangs, and other colorful individuals, all of whom have something fascinating to say about this experiment we call life. Both the boy and the audience gradually become aware that he has no more reason to believe that his "waking" life is any more real than his "dream" life.

One of the most fascinating parts of the film actually discusses, explains, and details the whole notion of lucid dreaming, a state in which the dreamer is conscious of the fact that he or she is dreaming and actually directs the action of the dream. For those who have experimented with this, there is a wonderful clue—which I won't divulge here—as to how we can tell if we're actually dreaming.

In the end, some of my favorite parts of *Waking Life* are its memorable, metaphysical lines of dialogue. Here are just a few of these moving examples: "To our neural system, there is no difference between experiencing something and dreaming something"; "Your life is yours to create. It's always our decision who we are"; that perhaps life is "just a dream," only as real "as long as they last. What if the same thing can be said about life?"; and "This is absolutely the most exciting time that we could have picked to be alive . . . and things are just starting."

When lines like these materialize in a film, I truly see how far we've come in our understanding of this thing called life. As an audience, we left "Kansas" a long time ago.

A Beautiful Mind**
(December 12, 2001)

The winner of the Academy Award for Best Picture of 2001, *A Beautiful Mind* chronicles the true story of eccentric mathematician John Nash (brilliantly portrayed by Russell Crowe) from his early days as a student at Princeton to his ultimate triumph over a descent into schizophrenia.

In a brilliant plot twist, we make a discovery about the existence of many of Nash's friends and cohorts. We note how he and Charles (Paul Bettany) develop a strong friendship as roommates at Princeton. We meet a shadowy FBI agent (Ed Harris) who recruits Nash to decipher complicated war codes. We see Nash haunted by Russian agents and targeted for infiltrating enemy secrets. And we meet Charles again with his beautiful young niece, who brings out a softer side in Nash.

But a massive breakdown reveals that all of these characters are figments of Nash's troubling battle with schizophrenia. This not only surprises Nash, but the audience, too. All of these "people" are simply manifestations of his psyche; they don't "exist" at all—at least, not in the "real" world.

Were you as stunned as I was? Those people sure look "real," don't they? And Nash certainly interacts with them as though they were real. Even on medication, he continues to encounter them, and even as he wins the Nobel Prize, they're "there"—at a distance, to be sure, but still there.

Nash's acceptance of the representations of his subconscious mind allows him to be able to cope in the world. The entities never disappear—he just learns to be able to differentiate them from the flesh-and-blood people around him, which is an extraordinary illustration of the very essence of coping.

Isn't this major plot device in *A Beautiful Mind* a perfect metaphor for the process of engaging all of our own inner manifestations and, yes, even demons? When we're meditating, just thinking, or even encountering the world, we hear those inner voices that interpret the events that unfold in our everyday lives. And we respond to many situations through the multifaceted mirrors of our psyche: A traumatizing event can send us back to childhood, or a well-adjusted adult can suddenly revert to awkward adolescent behavior when thrust into an uncomfortable situation. Those voices of the varied aspects of our being are as real to us in those moments as our friends and families are. Often, in fact, they seem *more* real, insistent, and trusted than our flesh and blood, and we may feel compelled by them to act in certain ways that we know are contrary to our nature. "The devil made me do it," right? (For those of us baby boomers who so fondly remember Flip Wilson. . . .)

It's only when we can differentiate such voices and compulsions that we can function from a place of true peace within ourselves. Much of the processing we do as adults on a spiritual path is focused on recognizing the moments when we feel compelled by childhood experiences or by something from our past. We learn to step outside them, recognize them for what they are, and refuse to engage in the behavior that those frightening entities seem to demand of us. When we can do that—in the moment—we feel a great sense of peace.

Just as John Nash experienced after he wins the Nobel Prize, we still hear the voices, but we recognize them for what they are, and we no longer engage them in "the dance." For me, that's the central and empowering metaphysical message of both *A Beautiful Mind* and Nash's real-life triumph.

Frida

(October 25, 2002)

Frida tells the extraordinary story of legendary Mexican artist Frida Kahlo and her relationship with her equally legendary husband, painter Diego Rivera, during the first half of the 20th century. Kahlo was one of the most powerful and fiercely independent role models for women of the day—talented, audacious, sexually liberated, nonconforming, and utterly courageous and fearless. Her paintings are striking, disturbing, powerful, and compelling—and so is the film. In fact, one of the most fascinating aspects of the movie is that it attempts to explain the origin of some of Kahlo's more famous and complex paintings. Julie Taymor was the perfect director for *Frida,* thanks to her visionary work on the stage presentation of *The Lion King* and her disturbing but visually brilliant film adaptation of *Titus Andronicus.*

The relationship between Kahlo (Salma Hayek) and Rivera (Alfred Molina) is the centerpiece of the film. They were fierce believers in liberation from all social convention, and they were also passionate lovers, for each other and for their world. Yet their relationship was marked by epic battles, separations, and heartbreak. Kahlo was the epitome of a brilliant and tortured artist: As a result of a traffic accident that literally shattered her body as a young woman, the rest of her 47 years were spent in great physical pain, yet it never stopped her from living her life to its fullest possible measure. And the tenderness and fire between Kahlo and Rivera offers one of the most fascinating portraits in recent memory of two extraordinary artists, comprising their lives, torments, and loves.

Frida was the dream project of many actresses for years, and congratulations go out to Salma Hayek for finally manifesting it! Her performance is one of those rare moments when you know that a performer was literally born to play a part—she inhabits the role as though she lived the life itself. And Alfred Molina as Diego Rivera is a revelation: It's just wonderful to see a character actor who has distinguished himself for years in smaller roles get the role of a lifetime and ace it!

Frida is not for everyone. It's an art film in its truest sense, it's rather lengthy, and it's also explicit in its sexuality. It does, however, illuminate the power of love and the soaring nature of the spirit of a woman who was a visionary—she set a standard of courage and determination that has resonated down through the decades. If you're drawn to the subject matter, then I believe that you'll be fascinated, thoroughly entertained, and absolutely inspired that this new age of feminine energy is actually being portrayed so thrillingly onscreen.

Far from Heaven **
(November 18, 2002)

Far from Heaven is a miraculous, beautiful, original, haunting, provocative, and extraordinary cinematic achievement—and that's not giving it enough praise.

Set in 1957, the film is shot as though it were actually *made* in 1957. Gorgeous Technicolor images fill the screen, and an evocative '50s-era score sets the stage—the result is an authentic experience that's dazzling to behold. (If you've never seen the leaves turn in New England in the fall, this is awfully close to being there.) The major impact of the movie, however, is that it explores issues that never could have been addressed in the era that it portrays.

The picture looks at the social and emotional fabric of the quintessential '50s family: Cathy (Julianne Moore) and Frank Whitaker (Dennis Quaid) are a seemingly picture-perfect duo living in a picture-perfect house on a picture-perfect street. A closer look, however, reveals a family very much on the verge of despair and suffering under the microscope of 1950s social and racial bigotry. Cathy's friendship with the family's black gardener, Raymond Deagan (Dennis Haysbert), becomes fodder for the gossip mill, and her husband's alcohol abuse raises a few eyebrows, most notably when "just one drink" lands him in jail. Then when Cathy pops in to Frank's office one night unannounced, she discovers him kissing another man. Yet she thinks that a visit to a shrink will "cure" him of his "despicable" attraction to men.

As *Far from Heaven* navigates the repressive terrain of the decade, I'm thunderstruck by how far we've traveled in the last five decades. We long ago established whites and blacks as equals, and interracial friendship is openly accepted today, as it well should be. Homosexuality is very much "out of the closet" now and hardly carries the stigma that Frank Whitaker struggled with (it certainly isn't a condition that rational people think necessitates treatment by a medical professional).

But more than all of this, we aren't afraid to discuss these topics anymore, and we aren't under the same societal pressures to bury these emotional issues beneath the surface. After watching this movie, I challenge anyone to feel nostalgia for the repressive sexual and social confines of the 1950s. *Far from Heaven* shines a bright light on that era, especially the painful cost of living in societal pretense. As the title so poignantly demonstrates, those "happy days" were *far* from heaven.

We sympathize with Cathy, Frank, and Raymond, but much of the beauty of the film is to look at just how far we've come. It's a celebration of the strides we've made, an accurate illustration of progress, and a toast to the power of the feminine. Despite being trapped in a male-dominated era, Cathy is courageous and brave (which was otherworldly in this repressive era)—the perfect illustration of the cinematic trend of embracing the new Divine feminine energy. Her courage steps outside of the male-dominated world, and to me, signals the birth of this progress.

Far from Heaven opens the doors and ushers in an energy we've been waiting for—guiding the way to the present day, where we take comfort and pride in the amazing spiritual, emotional, and societal evolution of the last half of the 20th century.

The Crime of Padre Amaro

(November 15, 2002)

This has been quite the cause célèbre in Mexico (and now around the world), but not for what you might have thought from the coming attractions, which focused on the physical relationship between a young, handsome priest and an even younger, attractive woman. Their sexuality is quite lovely and understated; however, the political aspect and hypocrisy of the Catholic Church is the explosive and fascinating core of this controversial film.

Some organizations have condemned this picture as anti-Catholic (when will *anyone* ever learn that such protests actually *help* business, rather than hurt it?), but it's really very careful in choosing its target. The actual conflicts and challenges faced by the Catholics in the film (which are the same ones we all face) are treated with respect, compassion, and dignity. In fact, every character faces a daunting paradox when their personal faiths conflict with the edicts of the Church they love and serve.

Since the characters are all intricately created, complex, and empathetic, I felt that the film, therefore, is most certainly *not* anti-Catholic. Some "sacred" positions of the Catholic *Church* are indeed challenged, such as the issues of celibacy, abortion, political power, and taking money from questionable sources. It is very revealing, then, that the attacks on the movie seem to be saying that an anti-Church position is synonymous with an anti-Catholic position; that is, the Church *is* Catholicism, and people who disagree should be damned (literally). This is the fascinating challenge that the characters actually face, so it's no surprise that the outcry over the film reflects the same bias.

The story revolves around young Padre Amaro (Gael García Bernal), who is assigned to the church of an older, experienced priest. While working there, Amaro discovers that his superior is building a first-class hospital with money donated by a notorious drug lord, and is also ensconced in a long-term sexual relationship with a woman who owns a local restaurant—this is not exactly what he was taught in seminary school! He also encounters other questionable characters, such as the most pious woman in the congregation who also arranges abortions for the right price, and a bishop whose political daggers are often buried deep in the hearts of his adversaries.

For me, the core of the movie illuminates the vast disparity between the tenets of the still-out-of-step Catholic Church and the realities of today's more progressive Catholics. The characters in the movie struggle to maintain their own faith and act in alignment with the outerworld edicts of the political machinery of the Church, but they just can't seem to justify within themselves why they're obligated to uphold these archaic practices and beliefs. It reminded me of how much life has changed over these last several decades vis-à-vis older archetypes of faith. *The Crime of Padre Amaro* serves to illustrate that *true* faith must always come from within, and that any attempt to structure and codify that faith is anathema to one's inner compass. I say "Amen" to that!

I believe that Spiritual Cinema reflects a deep longing in our universal consciousness for the identification and resolution of the issues that these films embody. One need only look at the sad and sordid scandals that resulted from protecting pedophile priests to see that the Catholic Church's hierarchy has lost much of the respect of its own rank and file. *The Crime of Padre Amaro* illuminates the difficulty inherent in such issues and shows how deeply damaging that kind of edict can be. If one wants to be celibate, great, but mandating it as a lifelong behavioral pattern for people with healthy sexual desire can lead, and obviously has led, to inner torment and outer dysfunction. The film also asks a very important question: What does a lifetime of forced abstinence from the pleasures of sex have to do with *real* faith?

A friend of mine who used to be a monk told me recently that, due to the Church's inability to attract women to convents, almost 90 percent of the nuns in the world will be gone within ten years. I'm sure that there would be thousands of women who would still like to serve the Church if the rules of behavior were less onerous. Still, it stubbornly holds on to edicts that have lost the respect of believers and continues to maintain the "law" that its particular belief is the *only* pathway to God. *The Crime of Padre Amaro* reflects the tragic consequences of that kind of dogma and is a fascinating and important film, one that I recommend very highly.

The Emperor's Club

(November 22, 2002)

Culminating in the disgrace of the Enron fiasco, we've seen what unbridled greed has done to the culture of America. In an era ushered in by Michael Douglas's infamous, immortal, Academy Award–winning "Greed is good" speech in *Wall Street,* we've seen where that has taken us, and it *wasn't* good.

From the emotional and financial sting of avarice, a desire has sprung from our hearts for films that bring us back to a place of *integrity.* There's a deep-seated feeling in the country today that begs for a return to matters of the heart, and to stop this insane, media-fueled obsession with wealth. We're hungry for a film that reinforces and illuminates our value system, and *The Emperor's Club* does just that.

For those of you who have put off seeing the film because you thought it's just a rehash of *Dead Poets Society,* don't worry—so did I! When you see it, however, you'll realize that it explores a very different territory than that wonderful Peter Weir film did.

In *The Emperor's Club,* Kevin Kline is at his very best (which says a lot, because even his "mediocre" is awfully good) playing William Hundert, an instructor at an exclusive all-male prep school. He teaches the classics with a great passion for that time in Greek and Roman history when so many of our modern values were molded.

The film's plot revolves around Hundert's encounters with a particularly troublesome student who refuses to apply himself. In frustration, he pays a visit to the boy's father, a U.S. senator who's totally unimpressed with the values Hundert so respects in the Greek/Roman era—as well as being completely uninspired to help Hundert help his son. The earnest professor politely reminds the senator that Greek and Roman society provided a model for democracy, which the framers of our Constitution called upon for inspiration. "But more to the point," Hundert goes to say, "I would think when the boys read Plato, Aristotle, Cicero, Julius Caesar even, they're put in direct contact with men who, in their own age, exemplified the highest standards of statesmanship, of civic virtue, character, conviction."

This conversation embodies and foreshadows the film's primary conflict: Hundert's desperate efforts to impart the value of integrity into a young a man who has been raised with expediency as his god. The denouement of the film is chilling and poignant, as Hundert realizes that his only mark on the world is in the character of the minds he helps mold. We feel his frustration as he encounters an entirely valueless generation, where one singular, selfish virtue prevails: that "the end justifies the means."

The spiritual center of the film is that conflict of integrity and self-respect, as it faces the challenges of "winning at any cost." This is a powerful and perplexing issue that we all face in the world today. The desire to succeed—to win—has been so deeply embedded in us that doing the right thing simply because it *is* the right thing to do is looked upon by many as the foolish and naïve practice of "losers."

This wonderful film directs a very bright spotlight on that attitude and exposes it as a shallow and unfortunate philosophy, thus serving to remind all of us which values are truly worth holding on to. I highly recommend *The Emperor's Club* as an inspiring reminder of who we really are . . . and of who we *can be* when we operate at our very best.

Solaris

(November 27, 2002)

Those of you who saw the original 1972 Russian version of *Solaris* know what an engrossing (if long and slow) journey it was. Thirty years later, director Steven Soderbergh stripped the story down to its essentials, and the result is a spiritual journey into the meaning of love and life.

It's somewhat impossible to describe the plot of *Solaris* . . . and that's really the point of the story itself. The characters can't figure out what's happening to them either—all they know is that they're orbiting a fascinating and mysterious planet/presence called Solaris where they encounter the people they've loved most dearly. The challenge is that these people are also dead. "And death shall have no dominion" takes on a new and compelling meaning here.

The movie's characters are challenged just to *feel*—to go with their hearts, not their heads—and that's why I find the film so powerful and noteworthy. We're all confronted with situations along our spiritual paths that seem to be conflicting with our so-called logical minds. Inevitably, I believe that we're challenging ourselves to do what Obi-Wan Kenobi urges Luke Skywalker to do at the end of *Star Wars:* to reach out with our feelings. The Force truly *is* with us, and when we accept it, we trust the faith we carry in our own hearts.

Solaris creates and sustains an unsettling and hypnotic mood that stays with you long after it has ended. This movie is not for everyone (see my note further on), but if it draws you to it—like Solaris itself draws people to it in the film—then maybe your own heart is compelling you to experience its own longing for expression.

Now a note about the marketing of *Solaris*. Those of you who have joined me at any of our Spiritual Cinema Circle events have heard me speak about Hollywood not understanding or trusting spiritual material. *Solaris* is a classic example: They tried selling it as science fiction, then as a George Clooney vehicle, and then as a love story—in so doing, the studio drew in the wrong audience every time. The manager of my local theater here in Ashland, Oregon, told me that scores of people asked for their money back after seeing the movie because "it wasn't what they thought it was." (Lots of people actually *walked out* of the theater when I saw it.)

To this, I quote that great philosopher Charlie Brown: "AARGH!!!"

Of course these folks were disappointed! They were lured by a marketing campaign that didn't understand or trust the audience for Spiritual Cinema. It's as if the studio just decided, "Let's get as many ticket buyers in here as we can before they figure out what the movie is really about." They focused on Clooney, thinking that he'd bring people in, while ignoring the fact that his fans might not enjoy this subject matter. But they didn't address the individuals who *would* really find the story interesting: *us!*

In a way, though, this is all great news because we're in the "swing between worlds" now. As my dear friend Neale Donald Walsch says, "When you declare yourself, everything unlike it comes into your space." I believe that by experiencing and effecting this change in the universe, we can consequently bring recognition to Spiritual Cinema as a genre.

Remember that we chose to be alive at this time, one in which we're watching the old paradigm die and are experiencing the birth pangs of the new one. It's not a pretty sight at the moment, but the dawn has broken . . . and we are waking to the light.

Adaptation

(December 6, 2002)

Have you ever wondered why your favorite book got made into a movie that bears little resemblance to it? Or why many writers have a reputation for being neurotic and just plain weird? Or how difficult it is to produce a creative work that satisfies your expectations?

Adaptation is one of the most audacious and wacky movies in recent memory. In fact, you might have to go back to *Being John Malkovich* for one with this much originality and humor. (No small coincidence, as both movies were directed by Spike Jonze and written by Charlie Kaufman.) In that earlier film, we went inside the mind of the title character; in *Adaptation,* we go inside the mind of screenwriter Charlie Kaufman himself—as well as the maelstrom of the creative process. Our journey through his hysterically tortured musings on his own misery actually reminded me of a comedic version of that line in *The Silence of the Lambs* where Clarice Starling is warned not to let Hannibal Lecter get inside her head!

In this film, Charlie (brilliantly played by Nicolas Cage) is hired to do an adaptation of a particularly difficult book. He descends into complete hysteria over it, and actually puts himself into his script as a panicked writer trying to adapt a difficult book! Along the way, the movie uses a plot device that bears a wonderful resemblance to another Kaufman—Andy—and his alter ego, Tony Clifton. Cage plays Charlie *and* his twin brother, Donald (a less sophisticated, intelligent, and ethical version of Charlie), whom Charlie desperately turns to for help on his script. (Those writing credits and the dedication at the end of the film . . . might they just be real?)

If all of this seems a bit daft, well, it is! *Adaptation* is one of those movies where you alternate between laughing until your sides hurt and shaking your head at its mind-blowing innovation. Real people, including actors Catherine Keener and John Cusack, director Jonze, and even John Malkovich himself, are woven in to the fictional narrative, as "real" life and the imagined life of *Adaptation* are melded into one.

The dizzying back and forth of what's real versus what's imagined is the hallmark of great Spiritual Cinema. At its core, *Adaptation* presents profoundly revolutionary perspectives on the nature of reality itself. As viewers, we're pushed to the edges of rational thought and forced to question what has happened or what is imagined, and to me, that's a good thing. Metaphysics extols the virtue of uncertainty, and I congratulate Charlie Kaufman and Spike Jonze for taking us there.

In the end, *Adaptation* is definitely *not* a mainstream commercial movie, and that's one of its fantastic strengths. But for someone with a fascination for the creative process or who wants to see what the Hollywood development process is all about, this is the best example I've ever seen on the screen.

To paraphrase Willie Nelson, "Mamas, don't let your babies grow up to be . . . writers!"

About Schmidt

(December 13, 2002)

There's an old saying that no one ever says on their deathbed, "I wish I'd spent more time at the office." Well, Warren Schmidt may have disagreed with that sentiment.

About Schmidt begins on the day 66-year-old Warren (Jack Nicholson) retires from the Omaha insurance company for which he's worked his entire adult existence. As he faces life without the job that has come to define not just what he does but also who he is, Warren realizes that he doesn't know what to do with himself. Thus, he begins an odyssey that, after years of numb detachment, reconnects him with his own heart.

About Schmidt is a beautiful, heartfelt, poignant, and bittersweet film that, as Spiritual Cinema, is also a brilliantly rendered reminder of keeping our priorities in order and staying in touch with our feelings. (In some ways, it reminded me of what might have happened to the Nicolas Cage character in *The Family Man* if he'd never been given the "glimpse" that led him back to his heart—he would have had a lot more money, but the ache would have been no less.) As Warren makes his way out of Omaha *and* his rut, he encounters some hilarious moments (including a hot-tub scene with Kathy Bates that is utterly wonderful), but he mostly becomes conscious of the loneliness that he denied to himself for so many years.

When his wife drops dead the day after his retirement, Warren isn't wracked with grief or thrown into utter despair; in fact, he's struck by how very little he actually lost. His wife wasn't a *real* part of his life—she was simply a housewife, going through the motions, just as he went to work for dozens of years to do relatively little of actual importance. On a spiritual level, this emptiness is a grave reminder of the importance of family and of developing ourselves outside of what we "do." If we haven't planted the seeds of intimacy within our family and friends, then when we go to reap our emotional harvest, we're going to come up relatively (pun intended) empty-handed. Sadly, intimate moments with our loved ones will have been lost because of our headlong plunge into a purely financial, work-driven existence.

As he reflects on the emptiness of his personal life, Warren memorably says, "I know we're all pretty small in the big scheme of things, and I suppose the most you can hope for is to make some kind of difference, but what kind of difference have I made? What in the world is better because of me?" Yet he ultimately discovers something else that can sustain him: a relationship, after all these years, with his daughter; and one—brought on by a late-night Sally Struthers–esque television commercial—with a six-year-old boy in Tanzania. Thanks to this long-distance listener, Schmidt pours his heart into letters for the young boy and begins the process of self-reflection and contemplation so utterly lacking from his early years in life.

Brilliantly directed by Alexander Payne, Nicholson seems to have been constantly reminded to just *be* the part, and his accomplishment is a tour de force in the truest sense of that accolade. The persona that is Jack Nicholson is larger than life—that impish grin, the devil-may-care, rumpled, "I'm having a great life on my own terms" attitude endears him all the more to so many fans.

I encourage everyone to see this movie, regardless of age or station in life, as I think it perfectly illustrates the importance of establishing priorities early on. Beautifully crafted as a story couched with regret, Warren Schmidt is the realized version of what happens when you *don't* follow your dreams, when the excuses of "I have to [fill in the blank]" are the foundation for your life. Spiritually, we all seek to find meaning in each and every lifetime, and while Schmidt is the personification of what we hope *not* to become, it's also a call to action for what we *can* become when we make conscious choices to live a life we can be proud of, one that's anchored in meaning, with family, friends, and love as our guide.

Mostly Martha*

(August 16, 2002)

*This film is purposely taken out of
chronological order due to its relation to *About Schmidt*.

Just as *About Schmidt's* Warren was lost in the
mire of his own worthlessness, *Mostly Martha's*
Martha is lost in her own self-importance. While
Warren knows that he's no one, Martha is certain
she's someone—consequently, she loses herself completely in her neurotic battles for perfection.

In this delightful film from Germany, Martha
Klein (Martina Gedick) is the respected chef of a major restaurant and has no time for anything but her
work, which she loves passionately. She is meticulous
in her gastronomic creations and even scrubs her
own kitchen at night; such dedication to her craft
has made her a sought-after and respected name
in the world of grand cuisine. The problem is that
she has absolutely no life outside the kitchen—she
sublimates her entire life into her work. Where other
food-focused films such as *Chocolat* and *Like Water
for Chocolate* have used food as a metaphor for engaging in life, *Mostly Martha* uses it as a metaphor for
escaping life.

In *The Hours*, Virginia Woolf says, "You can't
find peace by avoiding life." Similarly, Martha discovers that she can't find peace by avoiding the
world outside of the kitchen. Her life is irrevocably
jolted by the sudden death of her sister and the arrival into her home of her eight-year-old niece, for
whom she must now care. Martha is utterly hopeless
at communicating with the girl and knows only how
to feed her. But wouldn't you know it—Martha's
young niece is so crippled with grief that she cannot
eat even one bite.

Simultaneously, a new assistant chef is hired at the restaurant, a vibrant young Italian who's full of energy and joie de vivre, who forces the reserved and calculated Martha to live rather intimately with a very different side of herself. (Don't you love the way the universe works?) This man's entrance into her life challenges Martha, the consummate control freak, to find a way to receive and give love outside of the kitchen for the first time.

Mostly Martha is beautifully acted, engaging, warm, and witty. This movie, like *About Schmidt,* highlights the importance of valuing love and family over the banalities and trivial aspects of work. It reminds us that at the end of life, the most important thing is how well we've loved, and how well others have loved us.

I loved *Mostly Martha,* and I know you will, too.

Antwone Fisher

(December 19, 2002)

Antwone Fisher is the extremely moving and harrowing true-life story of a young man who survived a brutal and abusive childhood, subsequently transforming himself into a poet, author, and screenwriter. (In fact, I think that this is the only "biopic" I've ever seen that was written by the central character of the film itself.)

Antwone's father was shot and killed two months before he was born to an imprisoned 17-year-old convict and then put in foster care. The boy was regularly abused—mentally, physically, and sexually (we don't see the brunt of it, but we know what's happening). Antwone eventually grows old enough to join the Navy, where he has "inexplicable" bursts of rage that bring him to a psychiatrist who befriends him, treats him, and encourages him to finally seek the solace in finding his family and putting his tortured past behind him.

Sound a bit rough? It is. Antwone's initial journey *is* through darkness (just like in life, right?), but the outcome is dazzling. This difficult voyage is what makes the film so inspiring and uplifting on a number of levels. The young man's character was so courageous and his internal compass so powerful that he overcame every emotional obstacle that one could imagine in an early life. "It don't matter what you tried to do," says a determined Antwone, "you couldn't destroy me!" He's triumphant because he's "still standing" and "still strong!" And, he promises, "I always will be." Today, Antwone Fisher is a husband, father, and successful writer.

Oh . . . and he also happens to be African American. The director (Denzel Washington, in an auspicious and assured debut) and the entire brilliant cast are African American as well, but that's not what is significant here. Martin Luther King, Jr., once dreamed of a world in which black children would not be judged by the color of their skin, but by the quality of their character—and this is the signature accomplishment, great beauty, and spiritual significance of *Antwone Fisher*. Justice, pain, redemption, and hope are all color blind: Antwone could have been white, Asian, Latino—anyone or anything. It was his determination to transcend his background that lifted him to greatness, and the film's compassionate embrace of that desire is one of its most admirable accomplishments.

Along the way, the movie also has a lot to say about the channeling of creative energy and the human desire for "family," whatever form it might take. *Antwone Fisher* is an extraordinary work about integrity, grace, and perseverance. We need more films like this, and the world needs more people like Antwone Fisher.

The Hours**
(December 27, 2002)

It has been a long time since I've been as moved by a film as I was by *The Hours*. It's eerie, disturbing, exhilarating, unsettling, totally engrossing, *and* brilliantly written, photographed, scored, acted, and directed. And it had one heck of a powerful and emotional impact on me.

The Hours tells the interlocking story of three women in different decades, all playing out in the span of one day. Nicole Kidman plays famed writer Virginia Woolf in the 1920s, struggling with how to kill off Clarissa Dalloway, the heroine of her book *Mrs. Dalloway;* Julianne Moore plays Laura Brown, a housewife in the 1950s whose life unravels as she reads Woolf's novel; and Meryl Streep plays Clarissa Vaughan, a modern-day book editor whose life is deeply affected by the two women who came before her. Linking all three characters together throughout the decades is their relationship to *Mrs. Dalloway,* that remarkable work about the plight of women—including their individual battles with depression, loneliness, and heartache.

Clarissa's dear friend Richard (Ed Harris) is dying of AIDS, but on this day she's preparing to throw him a giant party to celebrate his landmark achievement as a writer. As it turns out, the remarkably executed device that ties the latter heroines of *The Hours* together is that Richard is the abandoned son of Laura Brown—who contemplated suicide alongside *Mrs. Dalloway,* but held on to her life in the simultaneous moment, in flashback, that Virgina Woolf decides not to kill off her heroine.

The film makes deeply thought-provoking observations about human behavior, one of the most powerful of which is our need to be whole within ourselves . . . no matter which road we've decided to travel in life.

Nicole Kidman's performance is hauntingly brilliant, and it definitively marks her evolution from being considered a beautiful woman who can act to one of the most accomplished and powerful actresses in film today. And the Academy agreed. Although Kidman is on-screen for only a few scenes, the depth, pathos, and heartache that she brings to her character is, for me, comparable to Diane Lane's career performance in *Unfaithful* and Julianne Moore's in *Far from Heaven*. (Throw in Salma Hayek's bravura depiction of *Frida*, and 2002 was one amazing year for actresses. And I didn't even mention *Chicago!*)

Moore is wonderful in another portrayal of a '50s housewife in *The Hours*, and Streep is her usual extraordinary self, as is the entire cast. The film is a phenomenal adaptation of Michael Cunningham's Pulitzer Prize–winning novel by the same name, directed with great style and intelligence by Stephen Daldry, and scored by Philip Glass, who has composed one of the most memorable and achingly beautiful film scores since *The Piano*. In short, this is a first-class production all the way!

As Spiritual Cinema, *The Hours* completes (with *Frida* and *Far from Heaven*) the trilogy that I feel celebrates both the ascension of feminine energy and our evolution from the Male Age of Pisces into the Female Age of Aquarius. And it's about time, wouldn't you agree? The internal structure of the progressive attitudes of all three women in the movie through the decades reflects this amazing transformation as well.

As the title of this work refers, in part, to the time we spend in reflection after the occurrence of a particular event in our lives, so has this film fascinated and affected me since I first saw it on New Year's Eve 2002. *The Hours* addresses so many complex issues about life—and death—that it's one of those somewhat rare adult features that begs to be seen more than once to truly appreciate the depth of its perceptions of human behavior. *The Hours* is a deeply moving, emotionally challenging, and often brooding picture that may very well unsettle some viewers. With all that in mind, I heartily recommend it to you as a cinematic choice if you're in the mood for an absorbing, haunting, and intelligent film experience.

The Core
(March 28, 2003)

On one level, *The Core* is simply a fun ride: Popcorn and drink in hand, you can escape for two hours into an entertaining and pleasantly diverting adventure. On another level, however, there's something more meaningful at work.

The plot of *The Core* revolves (pun intended) around the discovery that the Earth's liquid magnetic outer core has ceased spinning around its solid base core. This occurrence has thrown the planet into environmental chaos that will destroy the planet unless the core can be "jump-started." A team of scientists and other experts is recruited to build a ship that will burrow down and detonate nuclear devices that will cause a chain reaction and, hopefully, stimulate the liquid core to begin spinning again.

For me, *The Core* reflects a reminder to moviegoers that our planet is in both an environmental and political crisis. The film even addresses our creation of "WMDs" (weapons of mass destruction), and the disaster in the film itself seems to have been caused by our experimentation with one of those weapons, which is somewhat incongruously, but very significantly, named "Destiny."

A Mighty Wind
(April 16, 2003)

When I first heard about *A Mighty Wind,* I was prepared to ignore it or dismiss it as a bit of comedic fluff, but I'm glad that my first impression was wrong. The director (Christopher Guest) and ensemble cast from the hilarious *Best in Show* are at it again here, this time with a beautiful and surprising hidden message that touched me very deeply.

Guest also directed a wonderful film called *Waiting for Guffman,* and he is, in my opinion, a truly original and wonderfully comic filmmaker whose movies always regard their characters with great affection, even while they're being lampooned—and that's a trick worthy of Houdini!

A Mighty Wind focuses on the present-day reunion of three folk-singing groups who were popular in the 1960s. For those of us who remember those days, the film is a nostalgic and affectionate look back into a time when folk music coexisted with the early days of the Beatles' reshaping of rock 'n' roll.

The central plot of the film revolves around a duo called Mitch and Mickey, played with amazing heart, humor, and pathos by Eugene Levy and Catherine O'Hara (the same actors whose terrier won in *Best in Show*). Mitch was devastated by their breakup in the '60s (personally and professionally) and never recovered, while Mickey is happily married and comfortable. Mitch and Mickey's biggest hit was a song where at the end they always shared a trademark kiss. That kiss takes on a poignant and sentimental meaning as the film goes along—not just for duo but for the other groups as well—and for us as an audience. The kiss itself personifies the innocence and the gentleness of the whole "folk scene" from 40 years ago. (*Oy*—40 years!)

Will Mitch and Mickey share that last kiss or not? Well, you'll have to see the film to find out . . . and I heartily recommend that you do. If you lived during that era, or if you want to see what we were like during that time (the hair . . . the clothes . . . the "vibe"—was that really us?), you'll love *A Mighty Wind*. I certainly did.

Holes
(April 18, 2003)

Family films have changed over the years, and the next two I'm going to discuss, which were released almost simultaneously in 2003, reflect that evolving genre.

Holes is the film adaptation of the hugely popular, award-winning novel by the same title that captured the minds and hearts of the new generation of young readers that was originally—and still is—attracted to the *Harry Potter* books. (Thank you, Ms. Rowling, for getting kids to read again!) And the young men who come together in *Holes* also reminded me of a classic film adaptation of another novel from years ago, *Stand by Me.*

Holes is the highly stylized story of a work camp where troubled young men are sent to labor instead of being held in a juvenile-detention facility. A wicked warden (gleefully and archly played by Sigourney Weaver) and two henchmen (one of whom is delightfully portrayed by Jon Voight) run the camp, which is located in the middle of a desert. Legend has it that an outlaw buried treasure in this very area, so the warden forces the kids to spend their days digging holes to find the treasure. Two of the boys, nicknamed Caveman and Zero, also have their own connection to the legend, including a family curse. The film plays out the stories of the treasure hunt and, in flashback, the curse and the legend of the outlaw.

I see this book in kids' hands everywhere, and after having seen the movie, I think I see why: *Holes* resonates for young people who feel disconnected from the world in which they live. They yearn for something grander—a vision quest worthy of heroes—

and they find it in this story of the search for treasure and redemption in the desolate wasteland of Camp Green Lake. For me, the spirit of adventure illuminates a return to a time when being young was about having fun, exploring, and just being a kid. And in my opinion, fun—without the stressors and expectations of our "adult" world—is something we could all use more of in our lives. For this reason, *Holes* makes good Spiritual Cinema.

This is also a good movie for parents to watch with their children, since kids will enjoy the challenge of the adventure, and there's much to absorb for the rest of us. My guess is that the film will play somewhat better to young boys, but even though there is no "Hermione" with whom to relate (like in *Harry Potter*), many young girls will enjoy it as well. *Holes* is a bit too intense for very young children, but I think that eight-year-olds and up will be very entertained—and some wonderful dinner-table discussions will ensue!

It Runs in the Family

(April 25, 2003)

It Runs in the Family literally does run in the family: It stars several members of the Douglas clan, and it's in the recognition of the true family connections of the actors that the film has the most impact. I was reminded very much of the poignancy of Jane and Henry Fonda in *On Golden Pond* (although that was, in my opinion, a truly classic film on several levels). While *It Runs in the Family* is sometimes a bit slow, and strangely lifeless, there are underlying messages of the resilience of both the human spirit and the depth of family that are potent and beautiful.

Kirk Douglas had a stroke some years back, and here he plays Mitchell Gromberg (the patriarch of a family), who is recovering from the same affliction. He has a distant and somewhat combative relationship with his son, Alex (Michael Douglas), who has his own family with whom he's repeating some of the patterns that he had with his father. Michael's son Cameron plays one of his kids, and Michael's mother plays his mom in the movie—so this is a real three-generation family affair.

Kirk's performance is brave, wonderful, and deeply touching. His portrayal of a man dealing with death all around him—and fighting his own battle with a body that's failing him even as his spirit soars—is alone worth the price of admission, or in this case, the price of a DVD rental.

It Runs in the Family is a wonderful and unique experience for parents to see with *their* parents (particularly for those families who have recently experienced a death or an ongoing disability). The film is most effective when it reflects upon the dynamics of the family core itself—different people with different paths who love each other for their diversity, not in spite of it. As such, it's a wonderful picture for families to see together; however, despite a running plot point with a 12-year-old boy, it might not hold the interest of many preteens.

Spellbound

(April 30, 2003)

When I first saw the ads for *Spellbound,* I thought that it was either a rerelease of the classic Alfred Hitchcock film of the same name or a remake. Delightfully, it's neither: *Spellbound* is an absorbing documentary that follows eight kids as they prepare for and compete in the National Spelling Bee.

One of the big questions Spiritual Cinema asks is: Who can we be when we operate at our best? The dedication that these young people devote to their quest (including up to nine hours a day of studying tens of thousands of obscure words) is deeply inspiring and fascinating to watch. Parents, friends, and entire communities rally behind the kids to root them on their way. (One of the most hilarious moments in the film is accomplished with a single visual: A local Hooters bar puts a congratulatory note on its marquee—and misspells it!)

The boys and girls themselves discuss their word obsession candidly; one even comments that the preparation for the contest could be considered child abuse—except in this case, it's the kids, not the parents, who drive themselves so hard. In fact, some of the parents even lament that they long to take their offspring to the mall for some relaxation, but the kids just want to study!

Spellbound concludes at the national contest and, wonderfully, one of the spellers we've been following actually wins! In a time in which so many Hollywood movies portray young people as slackers, thieves, or worse, *Spellbound* is a refreshing reminder that our future is indeed in safe hands.

Finding Nemo
(May 30, 2003)

Perfectly timed at the start of the carefree days of summer, one fun studio film stood out as a beacon of hope in the summer of 2003. It became an early favorite for the Academy's newest category, Best Animated Feature (and went on to win the award). That film was *Finding Nemo.*

Now hold on, here: This is *not* just a children's film—it's the highest-grossing animated film of all time! Its subtext is very much alive, à la *Shrek,* and adults will enjoy the movie as much as kids. In fact, I went to see it alone and just loved it. My youngest daughter is now 18, so my days of having an "excuse" to see kids' flicks are over. Now that my grandparenting era is getting under way, though, I look forward to many more years of enjoying features with kids sitting beside me.

The title character (featuring the voice of Alexander Gould) is a clown fish who strays too far from his coral reef, is captured, and winds up in the fish tank of a dentist in Australia. His father, Marlin (the voice of Albert Brooks), with the help of the hapless Dory (the voice of Ellen DeGeneres), trails Nemo into the Sydney harbor and attempts a daring rescue. Nemo, meanwhile, plots his own escape with the other seafaring dentist-office captives. I can only imagine how many kids tried to "rescue" fish from their aquariums by flushing them down the toilet. You see, the trapped fish believed that being flushed was their one great hope: "All drains lead to the ocean." Well, sadly, most drains *don't* lead to the ocean, but to sewage-treatment plants where the fish . . . well, enough said.

Like *Shrek*, *Finding Nemo* has dazzling animation, wonderful humor, and action for the little ones, but it also contains wit that will soar right over the heads of all but the most precocious kids and land right in the hearts and minds of grown-ups. For example, when Marlin and Dory run into a group of sharks chanting an Alcoholics Anonymous–like mantra, adults will certainly have the last laugh. To wean themselves from eating fish, the sharks chant: "I am a nice shark, not a mindless eating machine. If I am to change this image, I must first change myself. Fish are friends, not food."

With beautiful underwater visuals, a heartwarming story, and a few laughs thrown in between, *Finding Nemo* warms the spirit, reminding us that Spiritual Cinema can be fun, too. (And fellow dads, with a single father as the hero, this is a movie for us!)

American Splendor

(August 15, 2003)

What a wonderful and enchanting surprise this film is! *American Splendor* is the true story of Harvey Pekar, a working-class "everyman" who earned a name for himself in the 1980s for his comic-book series, appropriately named *American Splendor,* which was based on his life.

You think Larry David is a curmudgeon in *Curb Your Enthusiasm?* Well, wait 'til you meet Harvey! This real-life file clerk in a Cleveland Hospital generally feels and acts like the world was created to personally torment him. As portrayed by the brilliant Paul Giamatti, Harvey is touching, relatable, gloriously grumpy, and utterly hilarious. His equally misanthropic wife, Joyce, is played with great humor and idiosyncratic glamour by the brilliant Hope Davis. Both actors should have received serious Academy Award consideration for their performances but, unfortunately, they did not.

The film chronicles the life of a guy who begins as an out-of-sorts kid who somewhat clings to the emotional version of that colic for the rest of his life. Harvey expects disaster at every turn and never truly grasps the meaning of good things—even when they happen to him. Late in the film, he has a close encounter with cancer (which is cured), and Joyce tells him that he has to be positive about his treatments. The anguish of trying to be optimistic is so intense for Harvey that he literally cries out that he just can't do it! He also can't imagine having a child, but in one of the movie's most touching moments, he learns that fate has a surprise for him there as well.

Now I know you might be asking, "What's fun about any of this?" The film has malaise, depression, and a man who generally believes that the world is out to get him. But this cast of characters is so eminently lovable, relatable, and down-to-earth that you simply bask in their presence for 100 minutes. And you just can't help but cheer for Harvey.

American Splendor blends a variety of techniques together, most notably the clever inclusion of comic-book elements to move the story along. Thought bubbles pop up in cartoon form, capturing the banalities of Harvey's internal misery, and captions scroll across the screen in comic fonts. Real-life images of Giamatti as Harvey are also juxtaposed with sketched versions, which are animated and come to life to mirror the actions of their real-life counterparts.

Early in the film, the narrative cuts to a couple sitting in folding chairs in an all-white room, offering commentary and insight on what's happening in the film. We soon realize that it's the *real* Harvey and Joyce Pekar! Real footage from Harvey's semi-regular appearances on David Letterman's show are juxtaposed with scenes of Davis's Joyce watching and waiting in the greenroom—and intercut with Giamatti's Harvey immediately leading up to, and then after, the interviews. It's brilliant! This is an innovative device that makes for an altogether unique and engrossing experience.

American Splendor has even more touching and wonderful aspects, such as the glorification of the film *Revenge of the Nerds* as an inspirational message. We are the champions, indeed!

The title of the film (and Harvey's comic-book series) itself is a wonderful commentary on the journey into the everyday lives of its protagonists. These characters are people we meet all the time in our lives and, for me, are entirely more representative of the heart of America than the high-gloss characters we usually see in average Hollywood fare.

American Splendor gives us hardworking people who long for their place in the sun *and* for someone they can love who will love them back. They're survivors of countless encounters with the ordinary ups and downs of everyday life, optimists (no matter what Harvey says) who strive each day to keep that positivity alive in the face of disappointment and even heartbreak. To be in touch with this "real" side of characters is to know ourselves, and to recognize our existence in the world as multidimensional people, good and bad. And that's one of the key components of films in the genre of Spiritual Cinema.

I heartily—and wholeheartedly—recommend *American Splendor* as a fascinating and original film in a time where this kind of innovation is rare. I really believe that many of you will love it, and I can't wait to see it again.

Under the Tuscan Sun
(September 26, 2003)

Spiritual Cinema asks two key questions: *Who are we?* and *Why are here?* It illuminates our human condition in images, thoughts, and feelings that inspire us to strive for who we can be as a species when we operate at our very best. When movies touch upon all those issues, they resonate deeply within us. Such was my response to *Under the Tuscan Sun,* which revolves around a subject rarely even approached in mainstream films: women over 40 who divorce, are divorced (or widowed), or who simply have chosen to be alone. (While I acknowledge that I might be wading into dangerously "politically incorrect" waters here as a man writing about this subject, I *have* raised four daughters—so, unafraid of anything, I will plunge forward!)

Frances (Diane Lane) discovers in the first scene that her husband has been cheating on her and, very quickly, is sitting in her lawyer's office. She learns that she's going to have to pay alimony unless she sells her half of their home to her husband—who plans to live there with his new girlfriend. Heartbroken and humiliated, Frances leaves her home with only three boxes of books and moves into a "newly separated/single persons from hell" apartment. Two of her friends surprise her with a plane ticket to take a tour of Tuscany, and they convince her to depart with this warning: Frances is on the brink of being one of those "shell cases" who never recovers from a divorce and wanders aimlessly through life forevermore. Although she's still reeling from her divorce, Frances nevertheless takes off for Italy.

Feel familiar? It just might. Divorce has become an unfortunate fact of life in America over the last 30 years, and countless numbers of women (and men) have been forced to redefine their lives after all that they've known dissolves. The movies have certainly touched upon this subject before, and there was even that urban myth referred to in *Sleepless in Seattle* that compared the chances of a woman over 40 getting married to the chances of being attacked by a terrorist. (Doesn't this also sound a bit like the lyrics to a country song? Except that Frances doesn't lose her truck.) Don't worry, though—as it is with the most painful and wrenching passages of our lives, *Under the Tuscan Sun* ultimately becomes a poignant, inspiring, and empowering reminder of the resiliency and determination of the human spirit.

In the wonderful film *Crouching Tiger, Hidden Dragon*, the pivotal metaphor comes from a "myth" about jumping from a mountain with faith and a "pure heart," and that's exactly what Frances does when she arrives in Tuscany and falls in love with an old house. When she ponders that buying it is "probably a bad idea," she reminds herself that she *loves* bad ideas. Frances throws caution (and every dime she has) to the winds (of change) and dives in. In a new country where she doesn't even speak the language—and with no friends, compass, or "master plan"—she plunges fearlessly ahead with an absolute determination to reclaim her dignity and her right to be happy.

As adults, most of us have faced the prospect—or reality—of losing everything we hold dear. (I personally plan to always have a few DVDs of this film on hand so that I can give them to friends who unexpectedly experience this kind of challenge.) These life passages initially appear to be so traumatic as to be even life-threatening, but as Frances ultimately says, "You don't die from a broken heart."

While I realize that some people may argue that point, the inspirational message of this movie is that life doesn't *have* to end simply because one encounters a major emotional roadblock. As spiritual beings living a human existence, we're ultimately defined by our choices. Thankfully, our lives provide us with certain opportunities to redefine and even reinvent ourselves by looking beyond the fear and pain of a particular moment to the possibilities of transformation and transcendence. *Under the Tuscan Sun* paints such a portrait, and I heartily recommend it as an empowering, uplifting, and inspiring cinematic experience.

Big Fish

(December 10, 2003)

Do you know someone who loves to spin yarns or tell a tall tale? Do *you* believe a word they say?

Now what if you found out that all their stories were actually true? Would it change your life to believe them? *Would* you believe them? *Could* you?

Big Fish is a movie about perception—both regarding how we see ourselves and the realities we create every day. It's a movie about "telling a story enough times that we become the story," which, again, is a fascinating metaphor for creating the reality of our own lives. In a strange and unique rhythm all his own, director Tim Burton lures us into the deliciously fantastic and exaggerated world of legendary storyteller Edward Bloom (the elder version is played by Albert Finney, while Ewan McGregor portrays him as a young man). While Burton's trademark tends to be a penchant for the bizarre (see *Beetlejuice,* the eerily animated *Nightmare Before Christmas,* the original *Batman,* and the peculiar classic *Edward Scissorhands*), *Big Fish* combines his characteristic visual world with a slightly more uplifting feel.

Edward Bloom is a traveling salesman of sorts, and he endlessly regales his wife, son, and anyone who will listen with incredible stories of his life on the road—wild, magical, fantastical tales of giants, ventriloquists, elephants, and Siamese twins. . . . As a child, Edward's son, William, is enthralled by these amazing adventures; as an adult, however, he grows weary of his father's legendary tale of catching the "biggest fish" in the lake. Will (Billy Crudup) is convinced that his father is "full of the blarney," and they become estranged until the old man is dying. When he visits Edward on his deathbed, Will asks his dad to tell him the "truth" about his life. Most of *Big Fish* reflects that tale—which is, in many ways, wilder than the yarns Edward has spun!

To go any further with the plot here would be foolish and counterproductive, since the film plays out in a nonlinear fashion that seems, as it goes along, to be more of a fable of our very existence than anything else. Metaphors and tantalizing moments about our own humanity are much more important here than a standard plot. For instance, as a child, Bloom and his friends all fear the town's "witch" (played, incidentally, by director Burton's companion, the equally eccentric Helena Bonham Carter). By looking into her glass eye, one is "allowed" to see into the future to the moment of one's death.

No one dares lock eyes with the witch, but young Edward bravely charges up and asks to see his fate—after which he serenely exclaims, "Oh, *that's* how I go." This awareness gives him confidence: He knows that he'll survive everything else that happens to him before that moment of death. He can be calm, knowing that he'll survive war *and* combat his life with equal parts confidence, clarity, and strength. (This brings up a great audience question: If you could know the moment of your own death, would you want to? How would you live your life if you knew exactly how it would end?)

The title of the movie refers both to being a big fish in a little pond and also to the great apocryphal stories about catching—in this case, actually *becoming*—the big fish that "got away." If that sounds a bit paradoxical, it is indeed meant to be.

I sense that people either love this movie or loathe it, and for me, that's what separates great cinematic art from the run-of-the-mill fare we usually get from the studios. So if you're interested in immersing yourself in the gentle, loving, fascinating, and elliptical world of a filmmaking genius, then I believe that you'll walk away from *Big Fish* enchanted and enthralled. I certainly did.

What the Bleep Do We Know!?
(February 6, 2004)

The mainstream success of *What the Bleep Do We Know!?* is nothing less than a significant cultural milestone. Spiritual Cinema is here, in a major way.

Made in a fascinating and utterly awe-inspiring style that combines documentary-like interviews, stylistic and exciting animation, and a dramatic story line featuring a character named Amanda (Marlee Matlin), the movie is an innovative masterwork of spirituality.

Filmmakers William Arntz, Mark Vicente, and Betsy Chasse deserve Nobel Prizes just for having the courage to attempt such a daredevil, high-wire act! It took them three years to meld this bracing blend of animation, documentary, and live action into a coherent and entertaining movie—and they have succeeded brilliantly. I was hooked from the very first images, beautifully photographed by co-director/producer and cinematographer Mark Vicente (the city of Portland, Oregon, should erect a monument in Mark's name!). The journey then plunges us into the ultimate questions of Spiritual Cinema: *Who are we?* and *Why are we here?*

Along the way, we meet several fascinating and eloquent scientists, authors, innovators, and spiritual seekers who discuss the basic secrets of our existence with intricate cohesion. Together, they make an inescapable and breathtaking case for the bedrock of metaphysical teaching: that each individual creates his or her own reality—that is, there is no objective experience of the world around us. We create all of it, including our thoughts, feelings, and intentions. This is the first film in my memory to illuminate that issue in such a frank, no-holds-barred fashion—truly, the calling card of Spiritual Cinema. I was so thrilled and amazed to witness these discussions up on a big screen, where the rest of the world could note what we seekers have known for so long.

Juxtaposed with the discussions and insights is a poignant and deeply moving story about Amanda, a Portland-based photographer who actually observes and experiences many of the issues presented by the personalities in the documentary aspects of the film. For example, she sees multiple versions of herself in different situations where a few little decisions here and there can reshape an entire lifetime. It's a wonderful way of demonstrating how deeply our own choices impact our lives.

Beyond all of that, however, Amanda's tale is also one of heartbreaking honesty and vulnerability, as she faces her own inner demons, rooted in feeling deeply ashamed of herself. Through her depiction of the debilitating effects of a negative self-image, Matlin's performance is so naked and vulnerable that it seems more like she's purging the depths of her soul than merely acting a part in a movie.

Amanda also meets Reggie (extraordinary young actor Robert Bailey, Jr.) on a basketball court (which is a great metaphor for the "game" of life), and the boy challenges her with a penetrating question: "How far down the rabbit hole are you willing to go?" He's literally asking her how deeply she wants to look at both her own existence and the mystery of everyday life.

Finally, tucked within the documentary and Amanda's story is fascinating, state-of-the-art animation that illustrates the very inner workings of our cells as they respond to stimuli from the outside world.

What the Bleep . . . is nothing less than a cinematic adventure into the very nature of human existence, and as such, it has the potential to bring these deeply spiritual questions into the mainstream media and dialogue. However, I find the title to be a little misleading because it seems to minimize our abilities as humans. We *do* have the capacity to know more about the illusion of life than we ever have before. It's not what we *don't* know, but what we *do*. A title that downplays that aspect of our self-awareness detracts from, rather than enhances, the message of the film. But this is a trivial quibble compared to the brilliance of the film.

Just as Mel Gibson did with *The Passion,* co-director/producer William Arntz personally financed the courage of his convictions (here with a spiritual rather than religious theme), and he created quite a grassroots stir in the Pacific Northwest. He deserves to be rewarded for his vision and bravery, as do all those involved with the film.

Miracle

(February 6, 2004)

Miracle is an absolutely terrific, heartwarming, thrilling, inspiring, and emotionally satisfying movie . . . and the metaphors and messages within it are incredibly timely and provocative.

Most of us who were around on February 22, 1980, remember the event upon which the story of the movie is based: the miraculous ice-hockey victory for the U.S. Olympic team over the previously invincible Russian champions. Al Michaels, then a young announcer for ABC, spontaneously exclaimed at the end of the game: "Do you believe in miracles? *Yes!*" That moment catapulted Michaels's career, and the story of this Olympic team became a touchstone for the times.

My question is: Do *you* believe in miracles?

Although this film is set 25 years ago, it eerily reflects much of what's going on in our country today. By the time of the 1980 Olympics, the United States had suffered some pretty severe blows, most notably the taking of hostages at the U.S. Embassy in Iran and the depth of the tensions of the Cold War. Economic issues were at a critical point as well, and we just didn't feel too great as a society. As President Carter said then, "For the first time in United States history, polls show that most Americans believe that times are going to get worse in the next five years, rather than better."

Sound familiar?

Today the issues (and the world) have changed: Russia is no longer a foe, but other countries and philosophies challenge us in several places around the world. Most important, the divisiveness in our own nation may be at its deepest levels of animosity since the Civil War more than a century ago. One need only look at the current level of political rancor to see how conflicted we are with each other and how vastly different our priorities are.

In 2003, when many of us witnessed the most exciting Super Bowl in quite some time, what became memorable about the event wasn't the game itself, but a monumental "malfunction" that split the country in two—and it had nothing to do with the New England Patriots or the Carolina Panthers. No, despite the stupendous level of play by both teams, and the contagious energy and thrill of the biggest football game of the year, everything was overshadowed by Janet Jackson's halftime mistake. Within seconds, the FCC was in an uproar, CBS was in an uproar, and conservatives were outraged: *A breast! A breast on national television!* Our society's reaction to this infamous halftime "show" threw a great, bright light on the schism that currently divides our nation.

Some saw Jackson's performance as the last shred of proof that our "moral fabric" has reached an all-time low, while others perceived the reaction as further evidence of our hypocrisy regarding sexuality, and our strange standards of approving violent images but not sexual ones. Still others felt that the controversy represented a ridiculous amount of attention paid to a glimpse of a woman's breast.

Whatever the viewpoint, it occurs to me that *Miracle*, "coincidentally" released in theaters the week after the Super Bowl brouhaha, reminds us that we're once again in a state of national malaise. Unfortunately, even a sporting event can't cure it *this* time. We need to look deeper than that for inspiration . . . and, in my opinion, we need look no further than to our own children. Our sons and daughters are indeed the future of our world—not the extremists at both sides of the ledger, nor those who mock everything about life, nor those who want to take us back to the past for virtues that the modern world has forever altered. No, it's the ones in the middle who are only beginning to spread their wings in a world that can seem so frightening and intimidating, where the only hallmark of "success" seems to be how much money one makes. And while that can be a valid benchmark of success, it certainly shouldn't be the *only* one.

I encounter many young people in my travels around the country (and I hope I have the opportunity to meet more as the years go by), and there's a sense in them that we have indeed lost our way—that we're not as focused anymore on making the world a better place for our children. We've become more absorbed in our own immediate comfort than we are in the future of our children.

This is the miracle of *Miracle:* that it can inspire the young people of today to strive . . . to hope . . . to dream . . . and to rise above any- and everything in their paths. At the conclusion of the movie, Coach Brooks (Kurt Russell, in a typically wonderful performance) says that the lasting significance of that moment in Lake Placid was not so much the team's ability to dream, but their ability to *believe.*

Despite our malaise and our somewhat misguided attention to breasts and malfunctions, I still believe in us as a species. And I still believe in miracles.

Super Size Me
(May 7, 2004)

Super Size Me is a controversial movie that's worthy of its place within the pantheon of Spiritual Cinema more for the conversation it engenders than for the narrative that unfolds on the screen—and it's really lighthearted, amusing, and fascinating to watch. Morgan Spurlock, the creator/writer/director/guinea pig behind this 2004 documentary, is a very positive, optimistic, and ordinary sort of fellow who decides to eat every meal at McDonald's for four weeks. And we get to join him as he chronicles exactly what those 30 days do to his health.

Not surprisingly, Morgan gains 30 pounds, becomes depressed, raises the toxicity in his kidneys to near-fatal levels, and generally feels awful. You see, not only does he commit to eating three square meals at the fast-food institution each and every day for a month, he must also agree to "super size" his meal *anytime* an employee asks him if he'd like to, and he has to finish every single bite. Oh, and he can't exercise at any point during his 30-day experiment. And for an added twist, his absolutely delightful and loving girlfriend is, of all things, a vegan chef who completely supports his mission, but is horrified to discover what this diet does to his health and the intimate aspects of their lives together.

To quote that immortal philosopher, Homer Simpson: "D'oh!"

Of course, no one is meant to eat fast food exclusively for 30 days (although, sadly, some people do), but that's not *Super Size Me*'s point. Morgan Spurlock actually begins this experiment as a response to a lawsuit that two young women brought against

McDonald's (they claimed that the chain was responsible for their obesity), with hopes that the results would further raise eyebrows in the nutritional annals of Ronald McDonald-land. And *that's* where a spiritual message leaps off the screen: *What in the world has happened to our sense of personal responsibility?*

Anyone on a spiritual path knows, or at least senses, that we create our own reality in each moment of our lives; this concept is the bedrock of almost all spiritual practices. It focuses our attention on our own motives, hopes, wishes, desires, intentions, and even fears. We manifest the realities to which we give the most energy, conscious or not, positive or negative. As a very wise and wonderful woman (who is also a gifted intuitive) recently told me, this is also why psychic readings are truly only accurate in the very moment in which they're discussed. Our futures are malleable to the extent that our consciousness and choices can change those realities in an instant of clear intent.

With this in mind, were those two young women mowing down Big Macs without the slightest inkling that they were responsible for their actions? Were they inspecting their expanding waistlines without giving thought to the dietary choices that got them there? And weren't those effects of their own making? As for the idea that a fast-food establishment could be "responsible" for the issue of obesity in some people's lives, I can only say, "Oh, please!"

Sure, there's a corporate obligation to provide nutritional information (isn't that an oxymoron in fast food?) for what we put into our bodies, and yes, Madison Avenue spends billions of dollars each year to sell us burgers, breakfast cereals, and soda pop. However, we're at a place in our evolution where we simply cannot afford to continue to deny the impact of our own actions. And although this next thought may not be terribly popular with conspiracy theorists, there is no "they" out there. There's no corporate entity that aspires to poison us and intentionally fill us with toxic tastes—there's only *us*. We create *everything* in our reality. Again, "we are the ones we've been waiting for."

Super Size Me is also a great movie for young people because they can actually see the results of overindulging in fast foods. (**Caution:** There is some very humorous dialogue about the effects of such chow on Morgan's sexual desire, so use discretion when watching with the really young ones.) That doesn't mean that we parents will stop hearing pleas from the backseat to visit the Golden Arches, but they may come slightly less often and with less fervor, and that in and of itself would be a major relief.

And then, we can sneak off in peace *by ourselves* and indulge in a burger and fries every once in a while, right?

The Day After Tomorrow

(May 28, 2004)

"Disaster" movies: Why are we so drawn to them, particularly when they involve massive planetary changes? And why are there so many films that suggest that the only way we can get to the future is to go through catastrophe first?

I believe that we have trouble envisioning a positive future because we haven't been able to evolve from our past. So-called disaster pictures contain cautionary messages about the ways we've destroyed ourselves for so many years—through technology, overpopulation, pollution, nuclear power, violence, natural disasters, and the loss of freedom—and they also serve as reminders of what we're committed to avoiding now and in the future. Taken just at face value, the messages of these movies could be perceived by doomsday "enthusiasts" as frightening; however, I experience them very differently.

Once you've faced a fear head-on, it loses its power. For example, if the warning light comes on in your car to say that you need oil, you stop at a gas station and add oil to the engine, and the warning light goes off. When seen from that perspective, "disaster" movies are actually about empowerment; that is, they exist to remind us of our understanding and promise to each other and ourselves that we won't allow any of these doomsday scenarios to ever happen again. The glass-half-empty approach would be to look at these films as harbingers of terrible tragedies that are about to occur; but the half-full approach sees the fears, acknowledges them, and simply determines that, however complex the engine may appear, adding oil to the crank case will keep the engine light off.

I see *The Day After Tomorrow* as an engine warning light, reminding us that we need to take every preventive measure possible to keep global warming from destroying us. We know that we've been experiencing noticeable climate changes over the last 10 to 15 years or so. As a native of Los Angeles, I can tell you that we used to have at least *some* kind of a winter there. Yes, "winter" in Southern California meant temperatures in the 50s during the day and four to five months of rain on and off, but it was *our* version of winter—it wasn't scorching hot most of the time as it is now. I no longer live there, but all of us who did (and still do) remember how things were, and see how different they are now.

So we instinctively know that global warming exists; therefore, we respond from our wallets and our hearts when a film comes along that explores the phenomenon—we're listening.

As to the "wallet" equation, the film is spectacular to watch and is worth seeing if only for its spectacular visual effects. The sequence of the sea sweeping into New York City (and a boat floating down one of the major streets in Manhattan), for instance, is one of the most jaw-dropping effects I've ever seen. The story itself is a bit on the weak side, but that's not really the point of this flick (or most Hollywood summer blockbusters, right?). Dennis Quaid plays a paleo-climatologist (look that one up!) who sees a big climate shift coming, although not as quickly as it indeed happens. When it hits, the world is slammed into a new Ice Age literally overnight, and he must journey through the snow to find his son, who's holed up in the New York Public Library.

Okay, so the science is way off—not even the wildest ecological pessimist believes that such a scenario could actually happen overnight—but, again, that's not terribly relevant, particularly to our hearts. It is indeed the "heart" equation that's at the core of the film's appeal—not necessarily the heart of the film itself, but the heart that beats inside us all. I truly believe that, on a subconscious level, we remember cataclysms from past civilizations that we didn't survive. And I believe just as strongly that we've chosen to be here on *this* planet at *this* time to assure ourselves, our children, and our eternal souls that we will *not* let that happen again.

The "engine light" of global warming just blinked on, so let's tend to it and turn it off. (Better yet, let's switch to renewable energy so that we never have to "add oil" at all!) We are indeed the ones we've been waiting for. The "real" day after tomorrow . . . is ours.

The Notebook **
(June 25, 2004)

Sometimes, a great love . . .

Wheras both *Sleepless in Seattle* and *Cast Away* let us know that it's possible for us to have *more* than one soul mate, in *The Notebook,* a *single* great love is the theme. The two protagonists seem fated for each other—the minute they lock eyes, the die has been cast, and you just know they'll be together forever. Sadly, in movieland, "forever" doesn't always last too long—it's often just a few days, weeks, or maybe years, but it does end (see *The Way We Were,* among other examples). For a select few, however, "forever" means exactly that. Obstacles, challenges, time, and distance be damned—love survives and blazes brightly throughout their lives. And it is that destined and eternal kind of love that breathes passion into the core of this beautiful and poignant film, which is the adaptation of Nicholas Sparks's best-selling novel.

Set primarily in the 1940s, *The Notebook* revolves around two ill-fated teenagers, Noah (Ryan Gosling) and Allie (Rachel McAdams), who meet and fall in love during one idyllic summer, only to be split apart by Allie's parents.

The story that frames the flashback of these "star-crossed" lovers has to do with an elderly woman (Gena Rowlands) in a nursing home suffering from dementia. Every day she has a visitor (James Garner), who reads to her from a book that tells the story of a young couple falling in love in the '40s. Much later on, we come to find that this couple is the elderly version of the young lovers. Noah reads their story to

Allie to bring her back from the grips of her disease, to help her remember him, their great love, and who she is.

The intensity of the plot magnifies exponentially with the incredible revelation that comes in the last minutes of the film, when we realize just who these two people are. As Noah reads the last pages of the young lovers' story, Allie reaches for him knowingly—it has all come back to her! She's there, with him, for just a few seconds. And that's when we see the inscription on the notebook and realize that Allie wrote the story so that Noah could read it to her once she forgot. I challenge *anyone* to maintain a dry eye while viewing this scene.

It's so beautiful to see this couple's love evolve over time, culminating in their "twilight years" and the challenges they bring to the relationship. More often than not, screen romances focus on the "getting there," but they very rarely illuminate the "being there" or, even more rarely, the "having been there." How many of us love to fall in love but are somewhat less successful when it comes to "maintaining" it? That's why we're so touched by Noah's endearing, enduring love for Allie, and for all that he does to keep it alive.

The Notebook makes us all yearn for that one amazing, incredible, earth-shattering, to-the-end-of-time love. The warm feeling of promise, of hope for that kind of experience, will stay with you long after you see the film. And when a movie leaves such a lasting impression, you know you've been "touched" by true Spiritual Cinema.

Before Sunset

(July 2, 2004)

We meet people at certain times in our lives for certain reasons. Although relationships with such individuals may not end up being permanent, as may be the case for the couple in *Before Sunset,* those encounters leave an indelible impression upon our souls. If you believe, as I do, that we travel in "soul groups," and that we have "agreements" with each other as to the ways we're going to help each other evolve from lifetime to lifetime, then you'll understand the connection between this movie's two protagonists.

Directed by the brilliant Richard Linklater *(Waking Life), Before Sunset* is a sequel to *Before Sunrise,* which was shot nine years earlier with the same director and two-actor cast. That earlier movie was about two young people who met on a train, and in one night, fell in love, made love, and promised to meet again. Nine years later, Jesse (Ethan Hawke) is in Paris for one leg of his book tour, where his lost love, Celine (Julie Delpy), is living and working as an environmental activist. She comes to his book signing, and they end up reminiscing about what they've been up to since they parted.

All this happens in the first five minutes of *Before Sunset.* After that, the film is a tour-de-force plunge into love, vulnerability, lost innocence, and longing—as well as the raw, emotional honesty of two people who are on this planet to touch one another. Never have I seen two actors so completely inhabit their characters more than Hawke and Delpy: They both give bravura, wrenching, witty, and devastatingly honest Academy Award–caliber performances.

(Although neither, unfortunately, were nominated for an award for their acting, the film did receive a nomination for Best Screenplay Based on Material Previously Produced or Published. Whew—that was a mouthful!)

Before Sunset explores moments of grace in which we meet others who inspire, empower, and stimulate us to plumb the depths of our souls. As Jesse and Celine analyze their brief, yet memorable, initial encounter, we're reminded that every coupling helps us grow and evolve, no matter what the outcome, and that each relationship propels us along our path, even if it means that ultimate love is shared with someone else. Jesse, for example, says that he thought of Celine every day leading up to his wedding (he's now unhappily married with a son), and he's obviously still drawn to her.

The film is a bracing mixture of comedy, pathos, drama, and brilliantly insightful dialogue, no small thanks to the uninterrupted technique Linklater uses—every single moment in the film is played out in real time. Every awkward pause, lingering glance, and small step that take the actors from one place to the next are all on-screen for us to experience, see, and relate to. And one of the hallmarks of Spiritual Cinema is that we identify with, and react to, the characters on-screen as if they were actually in our lives.

When the sun threatens to set, Celine reminds Jesse that he'll miss his plane, and we aren't sure what happens: Does he stay? If so, are they going to be together for another night, a week, or an eternity? But it doesn't really matter—the *possibility* of what could happen is the most important thing, and the *knowing* that no matter what time has to do with their relationship, their love will last forever in their hearts and minds. And for those who are open to this concept, and to what it says about our soul's dance with love, the resonance of Jesse and Celine is a revelation about the human condition.

I Heart Huckabees
(October 1, 2004)

I Heart Huckabees just may be the oddest film I've ever seen.

It just may be the oddest film *anyone* has ever seen!

I'm not sure that there's a simple (or even complex?) way of describing this movie, and I'm not even sure if I liked or loved it . . . was bored or transfixed . . . was stimulated or depressed—maybe all of the above? I can say for sure, though, that it's utterly innovative in its style and subject matter and, as such, has no historical precedent. Maybe it could be described as *"What's Up, Doc?* meets *Harold and Maude* meets *What the Bleep Do We Know!?* meets *The Simpsons"*?

It is, in a word, strange.

Loosely told, *I Heart Huckabees* is about Bernard and Vivian (riotously portrayed by Dustin Hoffman and Lily Tomlin), a husband-and-wife team of detectives who help people solve their "existential" crises. These two delve deeply into the psyches, souls, and very essence of their clients in order to help them resolve complicated issues. Their vision of life is positive and utterly metaphysical, and they live by this mantra: "We are all one." Yet their counterpart, Caterine Vauban (played by the esteemed French actress Isabelle Huppert), presents the other side of life.

While Vivian and Bernard try to find meaning and hope in their clients' lives, Vauban is cruel, manipulative, deceitful, and hell-bent on telling everyone she meets that life is unimportant and meaningless. In essence, the characters—and the audience—are plunged into nothing less than a metaphysical drama about what is real and unreal, positive and negative, right and wrong. And along the way, we meet an assortment of truly eccentric and sometimes oddball archetypes, all of whom represent various aspects of human integration and disintegration.

The last line of dialogue in this movie is so delicious, and such a perfect metaphor for the way we create obstacles in our own lives, that it's worth the entire journey of the film itself. I always remember the last line of *Some Like It Hot* as being the best ever ("Well, nobody's perfect"), but this one comes very close in its own way to matching that impact.

Please note that this film is *absolutely not for everyone*. Its "R" rating is well earned for language and some sexuality. For those of you, however, who are looking for something completely different, unsettling, entertaining, exasperating, stimulating, and challenging, give it a shot!

Ray

(October 29, 2004)

This movie has it all: passion, vision, courage, demons, conflict, women, dreams. But, of course, it has
something else that will make your spirit soar: *incredible
music!*

Ray is a searing, joyous, brilliant, and complex picture that gives new meaning to the term *genius*. Genius
is indeed the lifeblood that runs through both the film
and the man on whom it focuses, the extraordinarily
gifted—and tortured—Ray Charles.

Several months after witnessing his younger brother
drown in a tub of water, Ray Charles Robinson loses his
sight at age seven. But thanks to his strong and fiercely independent mother, Ray was never allowed to see himself
as handicapped. Early in the movie, for instance, the boy
trips over a chair. Rather than rushing to help him, his
mother tearfully stands back, forcing him to pull himself
up and use his other senses to regain his footing. Heeding
her command of "Don't let anybody ever make you into
a cripple," Ray utilizes that single-minded determination
to both propel and inspire himself to make music that no
one else had even conceived of.

Ray follows the driven performer through the 1950s
and '60s as he navigates the world of small clubs, un-
scrupulous managers, and initially skeptical audiences.
Through it all, he listens to the music in his head and
heart—and, in the process, creates a new blend of blues
and gospel that had never been heard before. Along the
way, he also seeks the love and solace of women to draw
him out of the darkness. Although Ray didn't rely on the
use of a cane or a seeing-eye dog to find his way, drugs

became a crutch of another sort, causing him to descend into the hell of addiction, which ultimately threatens his marriage, career, and life.

But the music! The film gives us the whole rainbow of Ray Charles's songs, from the ballads to the rousing blues/gospel anthems that made him a worldwide phenomenon. Those of us who loved his music (and even those who never heard it) are not disappointed. The music is *there* throughout this movie!

The picture never flinches from showing the multilayered complexity of the tortured genius that was Ray Charles. In addition, it is benefited by brilliant acting from the entire cast, spearheaded by a portrayal from Jamie Foxx as Ray that is purely transcendent. He *becomes* Ray Charles—the mannerisms, the music, the hearing of that distant drummer that propels him through the darkness. Simply put, Foxx steps into that rare pantheon of biographical performances (Barbra Streisand in *Funny Girl* comes to mind) that will define him forever. And an Academy Award for Best Actor didn't hurt to secure Foxx's lasting legacy either.

Finding Neverland

(November 12, 2004)

Finding Neverland is an absolutely magical, emotional, touching, and beautiful film that's full of love and enchantment. As directed by Marc Forster *(Monster's Ball)*, this picture illuminates the spirit of humanity and hope that so many of us yearn for when we go to the theater or pop in a DVD.

Set in London in 1904, *Finding Neverland* is loosely based on the true story of how Scottish author James Barrie was inspired to write and initially stage the immortal *Peter Pan*. Johnny Depp charmingly and lovingly plays Barrie as a man who knows that there's a unique place in his own heart—and in the hearts of people everywhere—where belief in magic is eternal. He calls this place Neverland.

Struggling after the flop of his most recent play, Barrie idles away his hours in a local park, where one day he meets widowed mother Sylvia Davies (the exquisite Kate Winslet) in the company of her four young sons. Sylvia herself is seeking a way to find a sense of adventure for her children that will help them deal with their sorrow over the death of their father. Barrie introduces her to his own vision of Neverland, to which she's powerfully drawn for her own secret reasons. Barrie is enchanted by Sylvia and her sense of love and openness, which seems so different from the chasm that has opened between him and his own wife (a frosty Radha Mitchell).

Barrie introduces the boys, the youngest of whom is named Peter (played by the extraordinary Freddie Highmore, whom Depp lured to star as Charlie Bucket in Tim Burton's 2005 reinvention of *Charlie and the Chocolate Factory*) to Neverland—a world of play and imagination—and begins to help them through their mourning. Through the magic and whimsy of Neverland, the boys wrestle with their sense of abandonment and grief and become the proverbial "Lost Boys" of Barrie's *Peter Pan*. The magic between Barrie and these four lads illuminates the screen in a series of dazzling, imaginative adventures. Barrie's special bond with young Peter draws them both from the clutches of depression, and it is here that the film finds the depth of its soul. By easing the boys' pain, Barrie engenders in all of them a sense of their potential as human beings. Thus, that timeless classic *Peter Pan* is born.

Barrie is a man so deeply in touch with his own inner child that it actually threatens his relationship with both his producer (played by Dustin Hoffman) and his wife; nevertheless, Barrie presses on with his quest to manifest a piece of literary art that would change the face of theater forever. The stirring musicals of Andrew Lloyd Webber might never have seen the light of a London stage if Barrie hadn't been so devoted to creating Neverland for his audience.

Depp, who portrays Barrie with earnest grace, earned an Academy Award nomination for the role (he ultimately lost to *Ray's* Jamie Foxx), and the film, rightfully so, also earned a nod for Best Picture (but it couldn't compete with Clint Eastwood and his *Million Dollar Baby*).

Loving, heartfelt, and lyrically beautiful, *Finding Neverland* is the kind of movie that "they just don't make anymore." Just like the audiences who've seen *Peter Pan* over the last century, this cinematic work allows (and indeed encourages) all of us to feel better about, and even deeply proud of, our own humanity. When a film does that, it touches the face of the ultimate expression of the art form itself, and we're offered a glimpse of our own remarkable beauty as a species.

The Phantom of the Opera

(December 22, 2004)

The film version of Andrew Lloyd Webber's wildly successful stage musical of the same name, *The Phantom of the Opera* is a melodramatic (in the best sense of that word), deliriously romantic, tragic (in the best sense of *that* word, too), and epic love story. It's also one of the most gorgeously designed, costumed, photographed, and directed films I've seen in a very long time.

The movie has both a new prologue and epilogue that weren't in the play, and they contribute beautifully to the story of Christine and her tragically obsessed admirer. Christine is a 16-year-old chorus girl (the same age as Emmy Rossum, the actress who portrays her!) in the Paris Opera House, whom the mysterious "Phantom" takes under his wing. Under his tutelage, her voice grows magnificently, and the Phantom falls madly in love, terrorizing the opera house until his beloved Christine takes center stage. Meanwhile, *she* falls in love with childhood friend Raoul (Patrick Wilson), until she's kidnapped by the Phantom, who threatens to keep her in his dark underworld for all of eternity.

The body of the movie is faithful to the play, while, at the same time, taking full advantage of the richer and more abundant medium of film. For instance, the Phantom's first foray with Christine into his grotto beneath the opera house is a breathtakingly beautiful and mystical visual journey, whereas onstage, most of it had to be implied and/or imagined.

The cast is amazing, particularly Rossum, who plays Christine with a deep sense of compassion, innocence, and gentleness. Gerard Butler's portrayal of the Phantom is

alternately powerful, menacing, tragic, and fragile—
and his voice just soars! (Webber actually required
that all the actors do their own singing, and not one
member of the cast was dubbed over, save for Minnie
Driver. But she had her own, brand-new Andrew Lloyd
Webber–penned piece to sing during the closing credits, which was also nominated for Best Original Song
at the 77th Annual Academy Awards.)

Rarely do filmed versions of successful musicals
rise to the quality of their staged counterparts; however, I must say that I enjoyed this *Phantom* even
more than the two different stage versions that I've
seen. And it takes its place in the pantheon of Spiritual Cinema as a tried-and-true love story, with a
good cry all but guaranteed.

The Upside of Anger**
(March 11, 2005)

The Upside of Anger jumps off the screen and into our hearts as a powerful whirlwind of emotions. Many people on the spiritual path find themselves struggling with "shadow" feelings such as anger—and if you're one of these individuals, then I believe that this movie will bring you useful insights about that emotion, as well as the more uplifting ones of hope and redemption. At the very least, it asks fascinating, provocative questions about family and the elusive emotion of anger, which most of us flirt with on a daily basis. (If you commute to work in a big city, then that sentence should probably say "hourly basis.")

The story revolves around suburban housewife Terry Wolfmeyer (Joan Allen), who awakens one morning to find that her husband has simply left without warning. With four daughters to raise, she slips—plunges, actually—into a world of anger and bitterness, and seeks the solace of daily bottles of vodka. Her fellow drunk and neighbor, one-time World Series hero Denny Davies (Kevin Costner), becomes fascinated with Terry and her family. And beyond just sharing a mutual affection for the drink, these two come together in a way that's *real*. Together, they create a fascinating and very adult love story that's strikingly original and compelling.

Joan Allen takes a woman "on the brink," so to speak, and plays her with every color of the acting rainbow, from tragic sorrow to soaring comedy, and she never misses a single beat. Not since Nicole Kidman in *The Hours* have I been as blown away by a portrayal as I was by Allen in this film. (Costner, too, has never been better.)

Rage is indeed a powerful force that can literally sweep us into its fiery grip and deposit us into a world where everyone around us reflects our own wrath back at us. The four young women (ranging in age from their teens to early 20s) who play Terry's daughters are each brilliant and, most important, illuminate the various manifestations of anger that can insidiously appear in our children, as well as in ourselves. (The girls, of course, all blame their mother for their father's disappearance.) Each daughter chooses her own path of passive rebellion that takes Terry to her wit's end. Perhaps more than any film in recent memory, *The Upside of Anger* brilliantly sketches the individual challenges that these four young women must face as a result of a single emotion from one of their parents.

Ultimately, the situation facing all the characters in the film turns out to be a moment of grace, one of those times in life when (usually in retrospect) we realize that our lives have been redirected by a powerful and seemingly invisible universal force. In her magnificent new book, *The Unmistakable Touch of Grace*, Cheryl Richardson defines these moments: "Every event we experience and every person we meet has been put in our path for a reason. When we awaken to this fundamental truth, we begin to understand that a benevolent force of energy is available to guide and direct our lives. I call this energy the unmistakable touch of grace."

Cheryl's book eloquently and lovingly details those moments both in her own life and in the lives of dozens of others that *all* of us have experienced at one time or another—moments that slip into our lives disguised as tragic or traumatic, and which ultimately result in significant growth. Ram Dass, for example, suffered a massive stroke several years back—yet he emerged a changed and reinvigorated spiritual leader who, as a result of the stroke, was gifted with new insights. In fact, in one of our much-loved feature documentaries from The Spiritual Cinema Circle, *Ram Dass: Fierce Grace,* he refers to it as being "stroked," referring to the way that God has touched him.

Although critics both loved and hated the ending of this movie, wherein Terry discovers that her cheating husband is actually dead, not ensconced in some blissful lovers' hideaway in Sweden as was earlier proposed, I'll tell you this: When a film gives us new ways of evaluating negative life experiences, that's good Spiritual Cinema.

Afterword

THE MOMENT OF CONTACT:
The Ultimate Purpose of Spiritual Cinema

Where will it all go from here? Time, of course, will tell, but from our present perspective, the future looks very good for this new genre in which we both labor and love so passionately. No matter what the future holds, though, the genre will grow through the ability of filmmakers to inspire audiences through moments of genuine, heart-to-heart contact. Those moments are what great moviemaking is all about, and Spiritual Cinema offers the greatest possibility for deep contact with any type of film.

We'd like to close this book with a story of the kind of contact we mean: the type that defines our genre and makes all the effort worthwhile.

Stephen: In an earlier book, I wrote about my 20-year journey through the labyrinths of Hollywood to make *What Dreams May Come.* It was an often exhilarating, often heart-wrenching process, but it was something I believed in passionately. The movie would eventually break more hearts (and empty more bank accounts) than mine, as well as winning an Academy Award and a legion of devoted fans. In short, it was a triumph, a disaster, *and* a lifetime of learning all rolled into one.

The dream of anyone involved in moviemaking is to create a moment of contact between the work of art and the person in the theater seat. From the hundreds of letters and comments I received from fans, I knew that we'd succeeded in creating *many* such moments thanks to *What Dreams May Come.* But there was one special connection I was blessed to make, one that I will never forget. It was the defining moment for me, when the reason why I'd always felt so passionate about creating the new genre of Spiritual Cinema all became clear.

After *What Dreams May Come* opened, a theater owner in the Midwest called with a request from a man in Milwaukee named Chuck Weber who had a terminally ill 17-year-old daughter, Amanda. She'd seen the previews for the movie on television and wanted desperately to see it, but she was too ill to get to a theater. Chuck was asking if there was any way that we could send a videocassette of the movie to him for Amanda to view in their home.

Now you can imagine how difficult this would be for a big studio like Polygram, with so much money invested in the film. To put a video out into the world is a big business risk; however, when I called to ask for their help, they immediately agreed, and a video was sent by courier to Milwaukee. (Polygram was *so* obsessed with the life of the videotape, however, that they insisted that the courier deliver the film, then *sit* with the family as they watched it, and then bring the tape directly back to the studio. When the courier arrived and saw the gravity of the situation—the young girl propped up in a hospital bed in the family's front room—he politely left the tape with Chuck and asked him to call when he was ready to have the film retrieved.)

Ultimately, I found Chuck's phone number and left a message on his answering machine that said we all hoped the film would be what Amanda hoped it would be. A few days later, I got a call from a friend of the family to say that the tape had indeed arrived, but Amanda had passed away two days later. I left another message of condolence, and two weeks later, Chuck called me back. He told me that his daughter had contracted a rare form of incurable cancer and had been ill for a year, during which she'd been very brave. At the end, though, she got a bit frightened—and that's when she started seeing ads for *What Dreams May Come,* which motivated Chuck to find a way to get a video copy.

Chuck told me that he studied Amanda while she watched the movie, and he noticed that her entire demeanor changed when she saw the painted-world sequence: She just seemed to relax. The next day, she asked to be taken out to a park where she could see the fall colors. Chuck thought that she might just pass away outside in the peace of that setting, but she eventually asked to go home. On the way there, she told her dad not to worry about her because, as a result of my little movie, she had a frame of reference for where she would go. The next day, she died peacefully in her home with her dad and her friends.

Chuck's words that day forever changed my perspective. He told me that he didn't watch the movie, so he couldn't comment on it per se; however, he did watch the effect it had on Amanda. "No matter what, Stephen," he said, "this film gave peace to me and my daughter in the last two days of her life. Never lose sight of that. Nothing else is that important, is it?"

I will never forget those words. To this day, I carry a picture of Amanda in my wallet, and Chuck has become a dear and close family friend. He was a single father, like me, and we have a deep spiritual connection. My daughter Cari is the same age that Amanda would be now had she lived. And after getting to know her, Chuck gave a lot of Amanda's clothes and other personal effects to Cari, and some to my youngest daughter, Heather. It's been years now since Amanda's passing, but we feel her presence with us often.

To deeply touch even one human life in the profound way that *What Dreams May Come* affected Amanda is the greatest satisfaction I could ever receive from my work. She reminded me again of what really is important in my life: not recognition or the trappings of a traditional definition of "success"—it's about the work itself and the empowerment and inspiration that can flow into the hearts and minds of those whom the work touches.

A brave 17-year-old girl and her loving father taught me the real meaning of my work. I promise I will never forget.

We're both professionally involved in the making of Spiritual Cinema, but first and foremost, we're fans of the genre, just like you. We want to be in the audience right beside you when the lights go down and a heartful, mindful film lights up the screen. And we want to walk out with you afterward feeling better about being a human being than we did when the movie began.

We believe passionately, as you probably do, that Spiritual Cinema can help make a better world, in which people practice the values of compassion, insight, and transcendence that are embedded in the genre. Thank you for joining us in this incredible adventure. We truly are all in this together, and we are grateful beyond words for your willingness to join us in creating the new world whose promise is at the heart of Spiritual Cinema.

Christopher Briscoe

Stephen

David Baker

Gay

About the Authors

This book is a collaboration between **Stephen Simon** and **Gay Hendricks.** Stephen Simon, producer of such classics as *What Dreams May Come* and *Somewhere in Time,* created and named the new genre of Spiritual Cinema. Gay Hendricks is the author of many books in personal and relationship transformation, including *Conscious Loving, The Conscious Heart,* and *Lasting Love.* Along with Kathlyn and Gay Hendricks, Stephen Simon founded The Spiritual Cinema Circle, which brings inspiring movies to thousands of grateful movie lovers around the world each month.

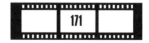

SPIRITUAL CINEMA
notes

We hope you enjoyed this Hay House book. If you'd like to receive a free catalog featuring additional Hay House books and products, or if you'd like information about the Hay Foundation, please contact:

Hay House, Inc.
P.O. Box 5100
Carlsbad, CA 92018-5100

(760) 431-7695 or (800) 654-5126
(760) 431-6948 (fax) or (800) 650-5115 (fax)
www.hayhouse.com

Published and distributed in Australia by:
Hay House Australia Pty. Ltd. • 18/36 Ralph St.
Alexandria NSW 2015 • *Phone:* 612-9669-4299
Fax: 612-9669-4144 • www.hayhouse.com.au

Published and distributed in the United Kingdom by:
Hay House UK, Ltd. • Unit 62, Canalot Studios
222 Kensal Rd., London W10 5BN • *Phone:* 44-20-8962-1230
Fax: 44-20-8962-1239 • www.hayhouse.co.uk

Published and distributed in the Republic of South Africa by:
Hay House SA (Pty), Ltd., P.O. Box 990, Witkoppen 2068
Phone/Fax: 27-11-706-6612 • orders@psdprom.co.za

Distributed in Canada by:
Raincoast • 9050 Shaughnessy St., Vancouver, B.C. V6P 6E5
Phone: (604) 323-7100 • *Fax:* (604) 323-2600

Tune in to **www.hayhouseradio.com**™ for the best in inspirational talk radio featuring top Hay House authors! And, sign up via the Hay House USA Website to receive the Hay House online newsletter and stay informed about what's going on with your favorite authors. You'll receive bimonthly announcements about: Discounts and Offers, Special Events, Product Highlights, Free Excerpts, Giveaways, and more!
www.hayhouse.com